TEN DAYS IN THE NORTH WOODS
A KIDS' HIKING GUIDE TO THE KATAHDIN REGION

For Mom and Dad, for introducing me to the wonders of the natural world.

—Hope Rowan

Text and maps © 2019 by Hope Rowan
Illustrations © 2019 by Jada Fitch
Photos by Hope Rowan unless otherwise noted.
Book and cover design: Teresa Lagrange

Published by Islandport Press
P.O. Box 10
Yarmouth, Maine 04096
books@islandportpress.com
www.islandportpress.com

All rights reserved. No part of this book may be reproduced in any manner without the express written consent of Islandport Press except in the case of brief excerpts in critical reviews and articles.

Although the author and publisher have made every effort to ensure that the information in this book was correct at press time, the author and publisher do not assume and hereby disclaim any liability to any party for any loss, damage, or disruption caused by errors, omissions, or out-of-date information. Always confirm information before making travel plans.

ISBN: 978-1-944762-64-3
Library of Congress Control Number: 2018964886
Printed in the USA by Versa Press

TEN DAYS IN THE NORTH WOODS
A KIDS' HIKING GUIDE TO THE KATAHDIN REGION

BY **HOPE ROWAN**   ART BY **JADA FITCH**

ISLANDPORT PRESS

AUTHOR'S NOTE

Photo by Kevin Bennett/Islandport Press

I wrote this guide in part to help you and your family navigate Maine's North Woods and its trails. An additional—and just as important—objective of this guide is to engage kids with nature. Studies show that spending time outdoors improves children's physical, mental, emotional, and social health, as well as their overall sense of well-being. In this age of technology and screens, pressure to fill time with organized activities, and increased anxiety over "stranger danger," children spend less time romping outside than ever before. Hopefully this book is one tiny little way to help remedy that—to demonstrate the wonderful things nature can offer and show how much fun it can be to spend time outdoors.

With that in mind, I created the fictional characters of Hattie and her family. In their first trip to Maine, they explored Acadia National Park and Mount Desert Island in *Ten Days in Acadia*; here, they explore the Katahdin region. Hattie's stories in her journals and her enthusiasm for hiking aim to help the young readers of both guidebooks appreciate just how much joy the great outdoors can bring. By describing the hikes through a kid's eyes, I hope to engage young readers in a more immediate and accessible way. Instead of having parents read a guidebook to them, these books are *for* them.

While Hattie, her family, and their activities during their ten days in the North Woods are fictitious, their vacation could be that of any family enjoying Maine in the summer. The trails, descriptions, maps, photographs, and resources in this book are all 100 percent real, and the ten hikes are described as accurately as possible, so you can use it as a guidebook as well as a source of inspiration.

So, enjoy reading about the adventures presented in this book, then tie up the laces on your hiking boots, grab a backpack, get out on the trails, and have fun!

—Hope Rowan

TABLE OF CONTENTS

My Trip to the North Woods	4
Preparing for a Hike	8
Important Hiking Tips	10

BAXTER STATE PARK: SOUTHERN SECTION — 12
- DAY ONE: Cranberry Pond — 16
- DAY TWO: Katahdin Stream Falls — 24
- DAY THREE: Grassy, Elbow, & Tracy Ponds — 32
- DAY FOUR: Sandy Stream Pond — 40

BAXTER STATE PARK: NORTHERN SECTION — 48
- DAY FIVE: Horse Mountain — 52
- DAY SIX: Howe Brook — 60

KATAHDIN WOODS & WATERS NATIONAL MONUMENT — 68
- DAY SEVEN: Barnard Mountain — 72
- DAY EIGHT: Orin Falls — 80

DEBSCONEAG LAKES WILDERNESS AREA — 88
- DAY NINE: Ice Caves — 92
- DAY TEN: Horserace Loop — 100

ADDITIONAL INFORMATION

The Essentials	109
Helpful Resources	113
Things to Do	114
Places to Stay	116
Food, Supplies & More	119
Acknowledgments	121

MY TRIP TO THE NORTH WOODS

Last summer, my mom, dad, younger brother Gus, and I made a trek to Mount Desert Island, the home of Acadia National Park, for our summer vacation. We had such a great time that we wanted to go back. In the end, though, we decided to explore a different part of Maine. Instead of going to the coast, this summer we headed to the mountains.

The North Woods of Maine is an area right in the very center of the state. It's not a national park like Acadia, nor is it even a

About the North Woods

This guide covers three areas of the Maine North Woods:

Baxter State Park, owned by the state, managed by the Baxter State Park Authority, and most well-known for being the location of Mount Katahdin, the state's highest mountain, and also the northern end of the 2,100-plus-mile-long Appalachian Trail;

Katahdin Woods and Waters National Monument, established as a National Monument in 2016, administered by the National Park Service; and

Debsconeag Lakes Wilderness Area, private land managed by The Nature Conservancy as an ecological reserve, with the highest concentration of pristine, remote ponds in New England.

▲ There are no fees for day use or camping within Katahdin Woods and Waters or the Debsconeag Lakes Wilderness Area, but there are fees for camping and day use in Baxter, and you need to reserve well in advance to camp (see page 109 for full details). There are two entrance gates to Baxter State Park: Togue Pond in the south and Matagamon in the north.

Photo by Melissa Kim

▲ Roads in this area are heavily used by logging trucks. Be sure to drive on the right, never stop on the road itself, and park your vehicle well off the road or in a pull-off or parking lot. Always yield to logging trucks!

▲ Before your visit, it's a good idea to check out the regulations for each of these areas on their websites (see pages 109-112 for details). From the websites, you can also get the latest information on any trail or road closures and learn about upcoming programs and events, which are held regularly at Baxter and Katahdin Woods and Waters.

▲ Millinocket, "Maine's biggest small town," is the hub of the region, and serves as the gateway to the vast network of trail systems, lakes, and rivers that make up the North Woods. It is a great place to provision up, have a warm meal before camping, and browse Main Street for souvenirs.

▲ If you are driving from the south, it will take you about three hours to get to the region from Portland, or five hours from Boston. If you are flying into Bangor, Maine, Millinocket is just over an hour from the airport.

single park. Some of the land is protected as conservation land, like the areas my family visited, and some of the land is owned by companies that harvest the trees, mostly to turn them into paper. There are not many stores or houses or buildings of any sort, or even many roads, other than gravel logging roads, across this large, broad expanse of forest.

Maine's North Woods have a very rich history. Trees were harvested from this area since before Maine even existed as a state, to be made into things like houses, ships, and paper. About two hundred years ago, logging was at its height in the region, with sawmills filling the towns and logging camps filling the forests. The men living in these logging camps, out in the woods for long stretches at a time, told stories about the creatures living in the woods with them. One such creature, the Will-am-alone, is a squirrel-like animal that quickly scampers around, gathering up poisonous lichen. It forms it into little balls and drops the balls onto the ears and eyelids of the sleeping loggers at night, causing them to have bad dreams!

I am glad to say I didn't have any nightmares on my trip to the North Woods, so the Will-am-alones must not have found me. Today, there is still logging in the area, but people also travel there for fishing, hunting, canoeing, camping, and hiking.

I had so much fun hiking in the North Woods with my family. It is different from Acadia National Park in so many ways. Instead of the ocean, you're surrounded by lakes and ponds and forests, and mountains much bigger than the mountains in Acadia.

There are big rivers—some that twist and turn slowly through the woods, others that flow swiftly and tumble down rock faces, every so often falling steeply enough to form thrilling waterfalls.

The combined size of just the parks we visited is much larger—almost seven times larger—than Acadia National Park, and there are not nearly as many visitors. Also, we were definitely more in the wilderness than on our last trip, which was pretty cool.

Our adventure in Maine last year had given me confidence about spending every night camping and going for lots of hikes. That was a good thing, because some of the hikes in the North Woods are more challenging than those I did last summer in Acadia.

I hope that by sharing my trip to Maine's North Woods with you, you will want to go try some of the hikes yourself, and that you'll be well-prepared after learning about my trip. Reading is just the beginning. The real fun starts when you create your own outdoor experiences. So, get out there, go explore, and have fun!

Happy hiking!

Hattie

PREPARING FOR A HIKE

Being well-prepared and taking along the appropriate gear will help keep you safe, keep you more comfortable on the trail, and ensure that you have a pleasant hike!

What to bring:

▲ Map: Carry a trail map that shows trail distances and elevations, and know your route. I've provided maps here in my journal.

▲ Compass: Combined with a map, a compass is an important tool just in case you become lost or disoriented on the trail. And be sure you know how to use it before heading out!

▲ Water: Always carry plenty of water. It's easy to become dehydrated—which will make you weak and woozy—while hiking, particularly in the summer.

▲ Snacks: High-energy food, such as nuts, dried fruit, granola, and energy bars, will keep your body strong and energized throughout the day. This is particularly important on longer hikes.

▲ Flashlight or headlamp: When you plan a hike, set a turnaround time to ensure you finish in daylight. But in case something unplanned happens, which it often can while out on the trail, you should have a light with you, so you can find your way even if it gets dark. Lighting from your phone will not last long enough to qualify as a flashlight!

▲ First-aid kit: At the very least, pack some Band-Aids! First-aid supplies should include antibacterial ointment, a bandage, ibuprofen/acetaminophen, and any other supplies that you think are important.

▲ Extra clothing: The weather in the Maine mountains can change very quickly, and it can get cold even in summer. Synthetic clothing that wicks moisture, like a fleece top, is good to add to your pack, as well as a rain jacket.

▲ Sun protection: Slather on the sunscreen if the sun is out, or even if it is cloudy, in case the sun comes out later (or stick the tube in your pack). It's smart to wear a hat on a sunny day as well.

▲ Matches or fire starter: Store matches in a waterproof container, or carry a fire starter such as a lighter, just in case there is an emergency and you get stuck out on the trail overnight.

▲ Sturdy footwear: Trails are rocky, and footing can be difficult. Hiking boots, or at least a sturdy pair of sneakers, will make for an easier and more pleasant hike and reduce your chance of injury or blisters.

▲ Litter bag: Carry all trash out with you. It's nice to have a separate bag for trash, instead of just sticking it inside your pack with your other gear!

▲ Bug repellent: There will be bugs! In addition to mosquitoes and the notorious Maine blackfly, deer ticks that might be carrying Lyme disease are found in these woods. Cover up, bring bug spray, and if you are hiking earlier in the season and are particularly bothered by bugs, consider wearing a head net.

IMPORTANT HIKING TIPS

▲ Stay on the trails, following the blazes and other trail markers. Going off the trail can be harmful to the environment and dangerous for you.

▲ Check the weather before you head out. This way you can be sure you have the proper gear and clothing with you. If it's going to be particularly nasty out, postpone your hike for another day!

▲ Know your limitations. You don't want to get to the top of a mountain only to discover you are too tired to go back down! The more you hike, the more you will know what you are and are not able to do.

▲ Familiarize yourself with and practice the "Leave No Trace" principle, which basically means leaving everything as you found it. This will protect the fragile natural resources and ensure others can enjoy it too.

The most important thing to remember is to bring along your enthusiasm and have fun! There will be times when you get tired or swarmed by bugs or stuck in mud. But there will be so many wonderful times, too. If you can power through those tough moments, you will be glad you made the effort, and will find that it is all worth it in the end when you reach that summit, jump in that water, or complete your hike!

Baxter State Park
SOUTHERN SECTION

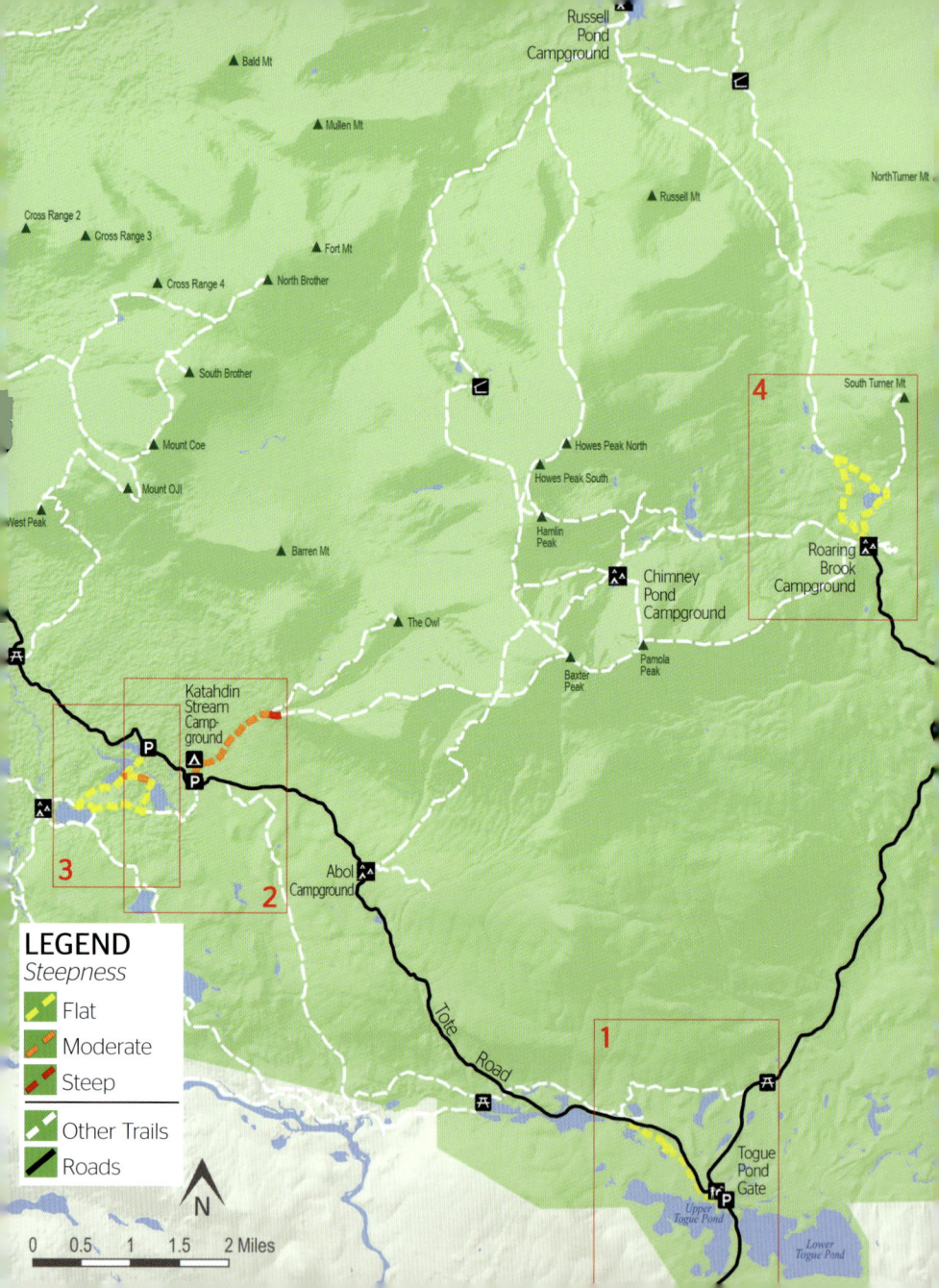

The original lands of Baxter State Park were given to the state of Maine by one of its former governors, Percival Baxter, in 1931, and he continued to add additional land (and money!) to the park over the years. He donated the land so that it would stay in its natural wild state. Today, most of the park is managed as a wildlife sanctuary (that's why no dogs are allowed). Mount Katahdin is one of its most noticeable features, but there's a lot more to explore within Baxter's 200,000-plus acres.

To get to the southern part of the park, you'll probably be coming from Millinocket, the closest town of any size. The last place to get supplies is at the North Woods Trading Post. From there, it's about 8 miles on Baxter Park Road before you get to the Togue Pond Gate. There are three campgrounds in the southern part of the park—Katahdin Stream, Abol, where we stayed, and Roaring Brook—that offer camping, with both lean-to and tent sites. There are two additional campgrounds that offer rustic cabins, if that's more your style! Be sure to reserve well in advance (you can reserve up to four months before your stay); they all fill up fast.

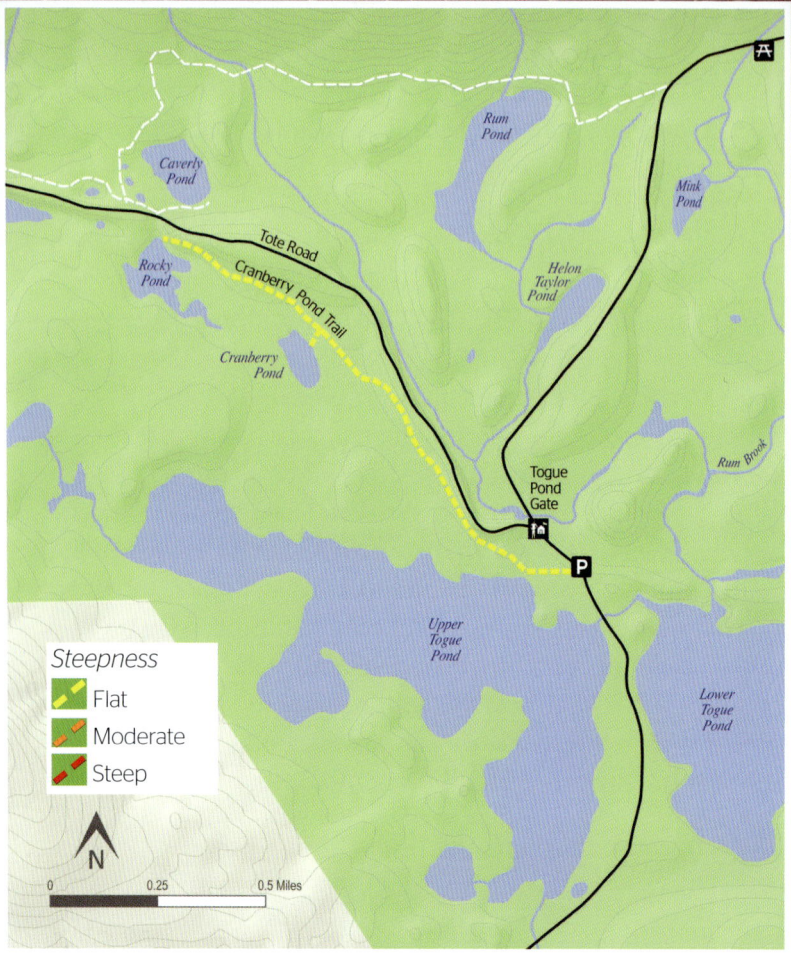

TRAILHEAD: The trail starts just before the Togue Pond Gatehouse, outside the park. If you are coming from inside the park, proceed a tenth of a mile from the gatehouse to a parking area on the left; the trail is across the road on the right. If you are coming from outside the park, you will come to the parking area a tenth of a mile from the visitor center, with the parking area on the right and the trailhead on the left of the road.

DAY ONE
Cranberry Pond

Total Distance
2.4 miles

Difficulty
Easy

Highest Elevation
710 feet

Time
1 to 1.5 hours

Bathrooms
Yes
Outhouse at trailhead

We arrived at Baxter State Park this morning. I was so excited for the start of our trip that I even enjoyed the car ride into the park. As we entered, we drove mainly through trees, though the road also snaked between some lakes. I put my window all the way down and took in the smells of the woods.

We made a stop at the visitor center on the way in. The ranger at the store suggested we head out back behind the building, and right there, across Upper Togue Pond, was an amazing view of Katahdin, which is not only the tallest mountain in Baxter but the tallest mountain in the state of Maine. It was named by the Wabanaki (Native Americans) and means "greatest mountain."

The ranger gave us some recommendations for things to see and do. Ultimately, we were headed to Abol Campground, a small campground in the woods with twenty-four lean-tos and tent sites. But before going to set up camp at our lean-to, before even going through the gatehouse, we went on a short hike to Cranberry Pond.

The trail began not far from the visitor center. As we entered the woods, we could see Upper Togue Pond through the trees. The trees in these woods were straight and tall, with needle-filled branches at the top, and not many branches below. I looked at the long needles that had fallen to the ground. They were in bunches of two, so I knew these were red pine trees.

Some dark clouds rolled by and it rained just a tiny bit. We hadn't brought our rain jackets, as there hadn't been any clouds when we started out. After that, we always made sure to bring rain gear along just in case. I was glad it didn't rain too hard or too long, because we would have gotten soaked!

The trail was pretty flat, so we could hike a little faster than if we were climbing a mountain. It didn't take us long to arrive at the sign for Cranberry Pond. The main trail continued straight ahead to Rocky Pond, and another small trail branched off to the left to take us the short distance to the pond. There was a bog between the edge of the forest and the pond itself. We walked on boardwalks over the bog; these boardwalks protect the bog plants and keep our feet dry.

There were some really cool plants in the bog, ones I had never seen before. Good thing we had brought along a field guide to help us figure out what they all were! I took lots of pictures of them, too, which has helped me draw them in my journal. They

Day One: Cranberry Pond

were all very different. There were sundews and cotton grass; there were pitcher plants, which had both interesting traps close to the ground and cool-looking flowers growing higher up, too; and there were lily pads in the pond.

We explored the edge of the bog for a little while, admired a hawk lazily soaring in circles high above us in the sky, and then crossed back over the boardwalks to get back on the main trail. Instead of heading right back to the car, we took a left to continue on the trail to Rocky Pond. This part of the trail was similar to the first section, although it did have a little bit of an up-and-down for us to traverse.

We found a spot by Rocky Pond to sit and have a snack, then returned along the same trail on which we had hiked in to both ponds. We still had to drive to the campground, check in, and set up camp for our stay in the southern section of Baxter.

EXTRAS: If you have time after the hike, you might want to swim at the sandy beach on Upper Togue Pond. This is a nice spot for a picnic lunch, too! The picnic area and beach are before the gatehouse and before the trailhead for Cranberry Pond.

FIELD NOTES

The **red-tailed hawk** is a large bird of prey that can be found anywhere that provides both high perches, from which it can look for its meals, and open areas for hunting. They like to eat small creatures like mice, rats, squirrels, snakes, and sometimes even other birds. It is the most widespread hawk in North America.

FIELD NOTES

Pitcher plants are carnivorous, which means they eat animals! In the case of the pitcher plants, the animals are bugs. Pitcher plants have a deep liquid-filled bowl, called a pitfall trap. Bugs go into the trap and can't get out because the sides are too slippery. The plant then digests the bugs.

NOTES

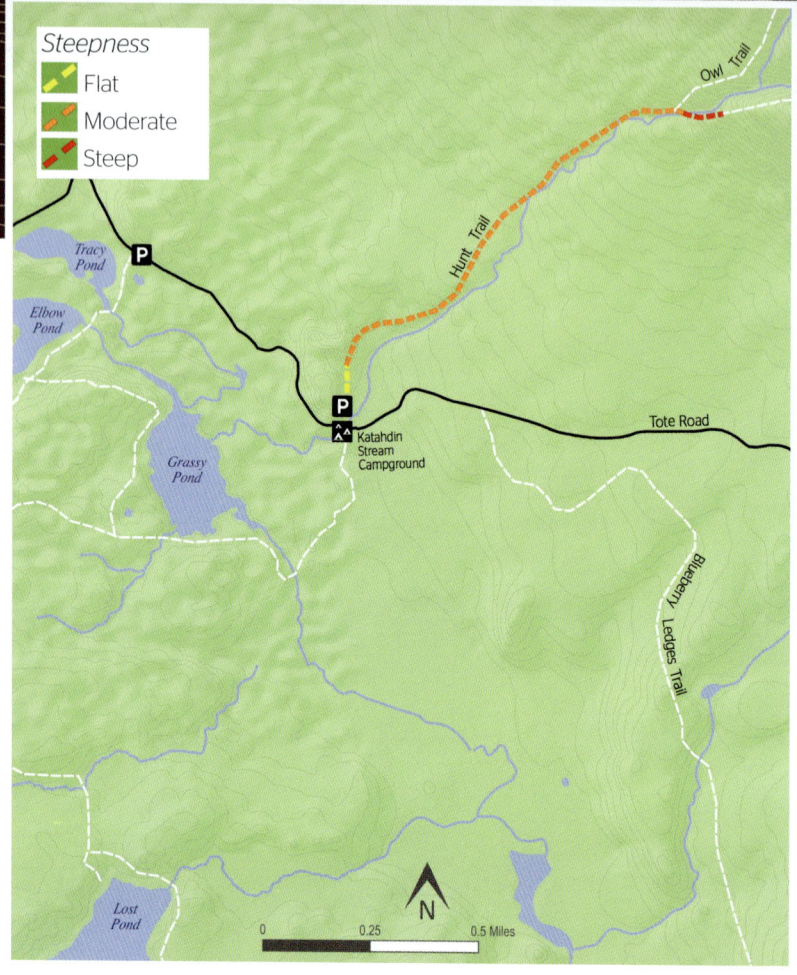

TRAILHEAD: From the Togue Pond Gatehouse, take a left at the fork. Drive 7.9 miles down the Tote Road to Katahdin Stream Campground. The day-use parking lot is all the way at the end, with the trailhead to all trails just beyond. Look for signs for the Hunt Trail. (*Note:* Because this is also the trailhead for a popular route up Katahdin, the day-use lot can fill up and close down early on, particularly on weekends and during the peak of the summer season.)

DAY TWO
Katahdin Stream Falls

Total Distance
2.4 miles

Difficulty
Moderate, with some challenging spots

Highest Elevation
1,600 feet

Time
1.5 to 2 hours

Bathrooms
Yes
Outhouses at Katahdin Stream Campground, and one at the trail junction just before the falls as well

Today we hiked on Katahdin itself. Okay, so we were just at the bottom of the mountain, not at the top, but still! We hiked to Katahdin Stream Falls along the Hunt Trail. This is one of the trails that goes all the way to the summit, and we saw a few groups starting their long trek.

Our hike to the falls was entirely in the woods, so it was a good one to do on a hot sunny day. Plus, there's always water nearby, so you can cool off by sticking your feet in the stream or splashing cold water on your face.

We started by walking along a short section of dirt path, where white flowers showing off in bunchberry patches caught my eye. After that, most of the trail was very rocky, which made for tricky footing. And where there weren't rocks, there were roots—lots of them! We climbed steadily, but there were only a couple of short sections that were steep. Even those really weren't all that bad.

Katahdin Stream was on our right, almost the whole way to the falls. Even in the few places where I couldn't see the stream, I could hear it rushing by. It's a big stream with lots of little falls, so it was pretty loud. But I liked that it was always there with me. Even if I had been by myself, the stream would have kept me company.

My brother Gus noticed that the blazes of paint on the trees and rocks that marked the trail were white. Yesterday, the trail markers were blue. Mom told us that the white blazes mean the trail is a part of the Appalachian Trail. The AT, as it's called, is more than 2,000 miles long! It starts in Georgia and ends right here in Baxter State Park. We were hiking on the very last part of the AT, before it ends at the top of Katahdin. There are people who hike the entire trail in one go, carrying everything that they'll need to camp out the whole way. They are called through-hikers, and it usually takes them about half a year to complete the whole trail. Maybe someday I'll be a through-hiker on the AT!

After we had been going for almost an hour, I knew we must be getting close to the falls. We came to a trail junction with a sign telling us that a mountain peak called The Owl was to the left, and the Hunt Trail headed right. We continued to the right, going down a slope to the banks of Katahdin Stream. We crossed the stream on a bridge made of logs. There were some falls above and shallow pools below. I thought these waterfalls were pretty cool, but they were nothing compared to what we saw when we came to Katahdin Stream Falls themselves, soon after that. We were looking down and across at them from a high bank. They were very impressive—and loud! My mom insisted on getting photos of Gus and me with the falls behind us, then a family selfie with all of us, and then photos of just the falls on their own.

On the way back down, Gus and I found a spot by the bridge where we could get to those shallow pools. We tore off our hiking boots and socks, and plunged our feet into the water. It felt so good, but boy, was that water cold! My feet instantly went numb. Then, when I pulled them out of the water, they felt all tingly—but in a good way!

After letting my feet dry off in the sun, I scared away the red squirrel that was hanging out on one of my boots, put my stinky socks and boots back on, and started back down the trail. It was easy to follow, since we were just retracing our steps back to the trailhead. Someday maybe I'll go all the way up the Hunt Trail—maybe even after hiking the AT—right up to the very top of Katahdin!

EXTRAS: We decided canoeing would be fun after the entirely-in-the-woods hike to the falls. Canoes are available to rent for $1 an hour. They are located at some of the campgrounds, like at Kidney Pond and Daicey Pond, and also at remote locations; check the park website or ask a ranger for more information. If you want to use a canoe at a remote location, you will need to pick up a key (many of them are locked), paddles, and life jackets from a ranger station and carry all the gear to the canoe. If you use a canoe at one of the campgrounds on the ponds, you won't have to lug the equipment, but you'll still need to stop at a ranger station to check in with the ranger and get your paddles and life jackets.

FIELD NOTES

Bunchberries are small plants with broad leaves that form a carpet-like cover on the ground. In June they have pretty, four-petaled, white flowers. Later in the summer, they have clusters of bright red berries. The petals are very elastic. They have spring-like structures that shoot out and fling pollen into the air.

FIELD NOTES

Red squirrels are all over the place in Maine. They first appeared ten thousand years ago at the end of the last ice age. Although they live in the woods and you're most likely to hear one chattering at you from a tree, they are very good swimmers. Small as they are, they can actually jump five or six feet straight up into the air; that's about as high as my dad's head!

NOTES

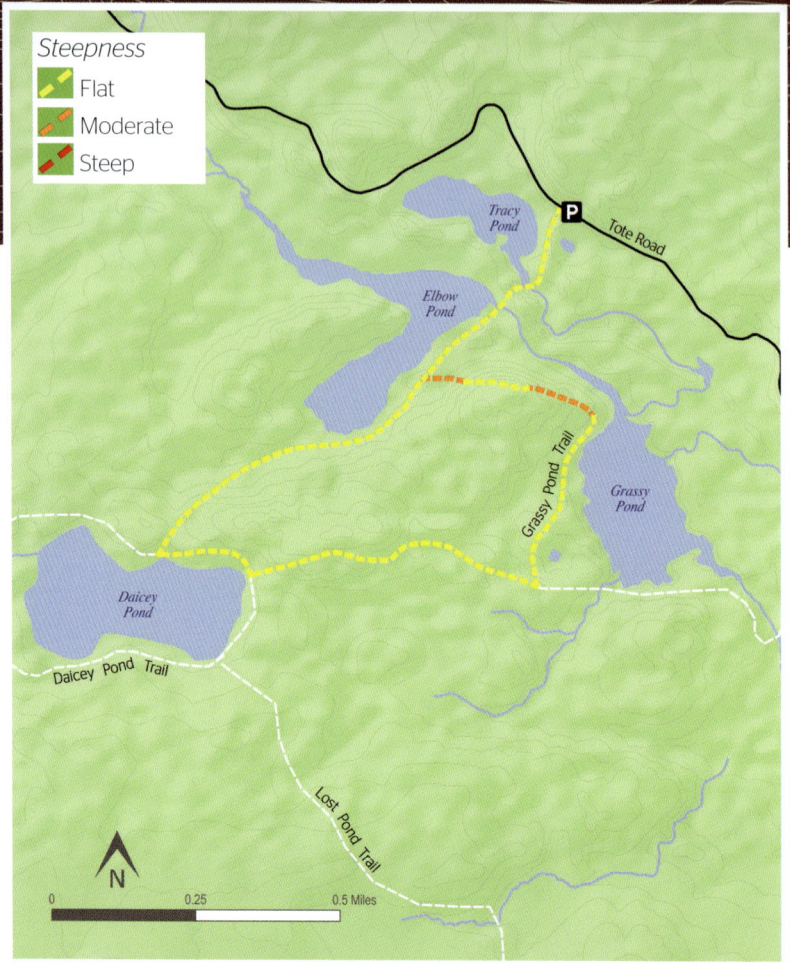

TRAILHEAD: From the Togue Pond Gatehouse, take a left at the fork. Drive 8.5 miles down the Tote Road, past Abol and Katahdin Stream Campgrounds. The parking area is on the left, with a sign indicating Elbow Pond parking and the trailhead just ahead. From the parking area, walk about 50 feet down the road to the trailhead, also on the left, marked with a sign for the Elbow Pond Trail.

DAY THREE
Grassy, Elbow, & Tracy Ponds

Total Distance
2.7 miles

Difficulty
Moderate

Highest Elevation
1,150 feet

Time
1.5 to 2 hours

Bathrooms
None

Today's plan: Wander through the woods and along the shores of several ponds, spot wildlife, and take in the sunshine and blue skies, and the amazing views from the ponds' shores along the way. Mission accomplished! This wasn't the highest hike (no mountain peaks on this loop), or the longest, or the shortest, or the most dramatic, but it was one of my favorites.

At the start, the trail went briefly through some woods. We then passed by a marsh to the right and crossed over the outlet of Tracy Pond. The bridge across the long span was only two boards wide, but it seemed sturdy enough. Looking toward the marsh, we could see logs with pointed-looking ends. My mom said they were trees that had been gnawed down by beavers!

From the middle of the bridge, we could see the peaks of Doubletop Mountain rising across the pond. We soon came to a second bridge similar to the first one.

After crossing the south end of Tracy Pond, we saw water again through the trees: Elbow Pond. If you look at the map, you will understand how it got its name. The pond is in two sections with a big bend in the middle.

The trees were really tall here and didn't have many branches—except at the top. So, although the trail was not right along the pond's edge, it was easy to see both the pond and the mountains beyond it. There were a couple of places where we could walk down to the pond's edge to get a better look. We identified the twin peaks of Doubletop Mountain to the left, the sharp peak of The Owl to its right, and then, farthest to the right, the large mass of Katahdin.

We left Elbow Pond at the first trail junction, taking a left to Grassy Pond. The woods here—and for most of this loop trail—were pretty cool. They were made up primarily of tall red pine trees, like we had seen along the Cranberry Pond trail. These coniferous trees—trees with needles, that are green year-round—have really rough bark, and long, thick needles in bunches of two. Here, same as at Elbow Pond, they were really tall, with few branches except near their tops, so that it was very open underneath, giving us good views and letting in plenty of sunshine.

On the way to Grassy Pond, there was a little bit of up-and-down as we went over small hills, but it was nothing like

Day Three: Grassy, Elbow, & Tracy Ponds

climbing up a mountain. Grassy Pond appeared through the woods on our left as we came down one of these hills. There was a ton of moss along the trail here. When it took a bend to the right, a short spur trail straight ahead took us to the marshy, mossy edges of Grassy Pond.

At the next trail junction, we took a right, heading toward Daicey Pond. The blazes of paint on the trees to mark the trail were white instead of blue again; we were back on the Appalachian Trail.

At the next trail junction, we had to choose: left or straight. Both would take us around Daicey Pond, but going left would add about a mile to our walk. So, we went straight, which led us along Daicey's shore for just a short distance before bringing us to yet another junction, where we turned right to head back to Elbow Pond. The trail took us along the shoreline of Elbow, on our left. We passed a canoe on its banks. If we had stopped at a ranger station to pick up a key, paddles, and life jackets, and carried them with us, we could have gone canoeing on Elbow Pond.

Our arrival at the next trail junction completed the loop, with just the short spur trail across Tracy Pond outlet to finish the whole hike. It was such a nice day out, Mom and Dad let Gus and me play at the water's edge at the Tracy Pond outlet to look for critters. Finally, we walked back to the car and headed back to our lean-to at the campground. What a great day!

FIELD NOTES

Beavers gnaw down trees to build dams of wood and mud, in order to create pools of still, deep water. These pools protect them from predators and allow them to float food and additional building materials across the water's surface.

EXTRAS: Can't get enough of these awesome ponds? If you take a left at the trail junction when you get to Daicey Pond, you can go all the way around the pond, on the Daicey Pond Nature Trail, adding 1.1 miles to the total loop.

FIELD NOTES

Sphagnum moss grows in thick, clumpy mats in bogs and conifer forests. It has been used for a really long time as a material for dressing wounds. Putting moss on a wound will help heal and protect it. In bogs that are made up mostly of sphagnum moss, the sphagnum has been known to preserve human bodies from millions of years ago.

NOTES

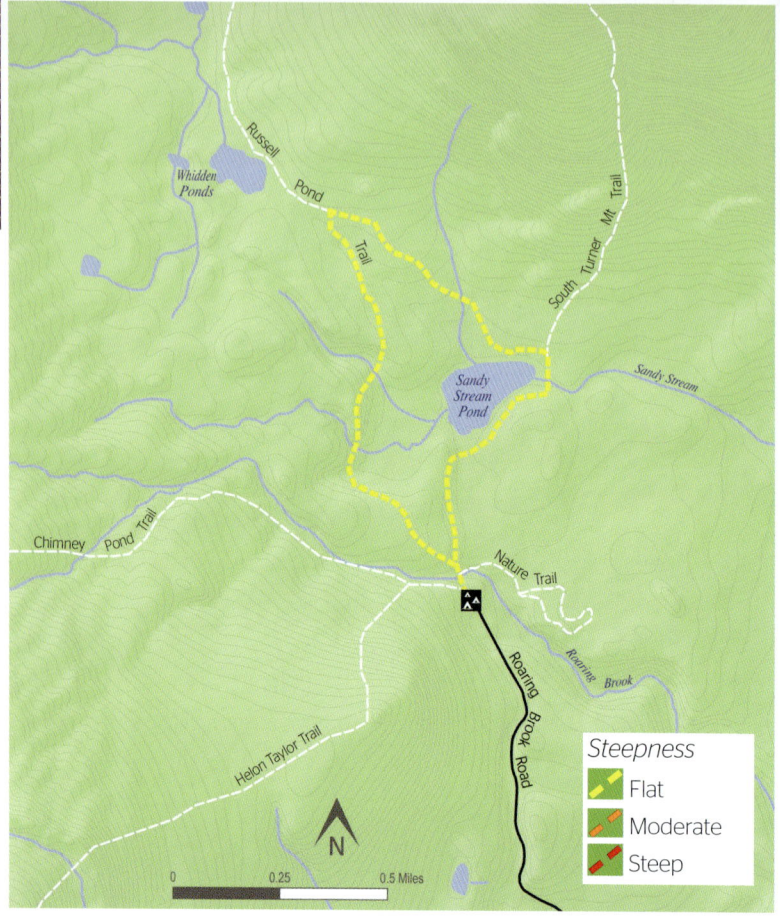

TRAILHEAD: From the Togue Pond Gatehouse, take a right at the fork. Drive 8 miles down the Roaring Brook Road to Roaring Brook Campground. The day-use parking lot is to the left, with the trailhead to all trails starting by the ranger station. Look for the sign marked Russell Pond Trail. (*Note*: Because this is also the trailhead for two routes to Katahdin—Chimney Pond and Helon Taylor—the day-use lot can fill up and close down early on, particularly on weekends and at the peak of the summer season.)

DAY FOUR
Sandy Stream Pond

Total Distance
2.4 miles

Difficulty
Easy to the pond; a couple of moderate rocky places around the loop

Highest Elevation
1,620 feet

Time
1.5 to 2 hours

Bathrooms
Yes
Outhouses at Roaring Brook Campground

I've never seen moose before, but there are many of them in Maine's North Woods. I was really hoping to see one during our vacation. A ranger at Baxter's visitor center told my parents that our best chance of seeing moose was at Sandy Stream Pond, so we got up very early in the morning to get there. We didn't make it quite in time for sunrise, but we were close!

All four of us headed out from the trailhead with high hopes of a moose sighting. Dad kept telling Gus and me not to be disappointed if there were no moose at the pond, to enjoy the nice walk and all that was around us.

Just past the trailhead we crossed a bridge over Roaring Brook, and then went right at the first trail junction toward Sandy Stream Pond. Our route had us making a counterclockwise loop around the pond. Along the short distance to the pond, signs asked us to stay on the boardwalks to protect the wildlife. There is a lot more wildlife here than just moose, so we respected the signs and stuck to the boardwalks. It was much easier than climbing over rocks and roots.

There were three paths from the trail to viewpoints on the pond. At the first viewpoint, there was a big platform at the water's edge. Three men were already there, even that early in the morning, with huge cameras set up on tripods. We weren't the only ones hoping for a moose sighting! My parents talked to the photographers while Gus and I carefully scanned the pond for the big creatures, but we didn't see any. What we did see, however, was Katahdin right above us. The mountain looked gigantic! It's so big it even has two different peaks that are part of the same mountain.

There was no wind that early in the morning, and the water was so calm and smooth I felt like I could step out onto the pond and slide all the way across on its glassy surface. The peaks of Katahdin reflected so clearly in the water that it looked like there was another set of mountains below the real ones, just upside down.

We moved on to the next viewpoint, called "Big Rock," because, well, there is a *really* big rock jutting out into the pond. It is mostly flat—a great platform for moose watching. But, once again, there were no moose to watch.

The third viewpoint was in a little marshy cove with a smaller wooden platform. As we approached, I heard splashing and expected to see a duck in the water. I looked out at the pond, and

I saw . . . a moose! It was so big! Mom said it was a cow, which is a female moose. Gus was so excited he made lots of noise, and I thought he would scare her away, but the moose barely seemed to notice. After raising her head for a moment in our general direction, she went back to snacking on the plants and roots under the water and slowly made her way toward us. We all watched her nosing around in the water for ages. Mom took tons and tons of photos. Eventually the moose wandered away, and we decided we had to keep on going if we were to complete our planned loop.

Once back on the main trail, we came to signs indicating the South Turner Mountain Trail straight ahead, and Sandy Stream Pond Trail to the left, so we went left. I could sort of see the pond through the trees, and once in a while I'd see something in the pond that I thought was a moose, but it was always just a big rock. When we came to a sign indicating we had reached the Russell Pond Trail, we took a left again, heading back to Roaring Brook Campground.

After crossing a small stream, we heard noises in the forest, and upon peering through the trees, I almost couldn't believe my eyes. It was another moose! It had antlers and was darker and larger than the one we had seen earlier, so we knew it was a male—a bull moose. We had spent so much time at the pond earlier that we didn't have too much time to watch it, since it was getting late.

The next time I heard the sound of rushing water, it was Roaring Brook. We were back where we had started, at the campground. I'm so happy to have finally seen a moose!

FIELD NOTES

Moose get their name from an Algonquin (Native American) word meaning "twig-eater." They have to eat forty to fifty pounds of plants each day. Bull moose, the males, can weigh up to 1,200 pounds. Moose have long flaps of skin hanging from their lower jaws, called the bell or dewlap. Different moose have such different dewlaps that it's a good way to tell individuals apart. Nobody knows why moose have dewlaps, or what they are for.

Day Four: Sandy Stream Pond

FIELD NOTES

Sugar maples can live up to two hundred years, or even longer. The sugar maple has the most sugar content in its sap of any of the maple species, and for that reason it's often tapped to make maple syrup. It takes about forty gallons of sap to make just a single gallon of syrup.

NOTES

EXTRAS: The short Nature Trail, also beginning at Roaring Brook Campground, offers some great photo ops of Roaring Brook, before the trail heads off into the woods, looping through a spruce forest. It also offers mountain views over a bog, with two viewing platforms at the edge of the bog. Mom and I did this after our hike; there was a lot to see on a short loop!

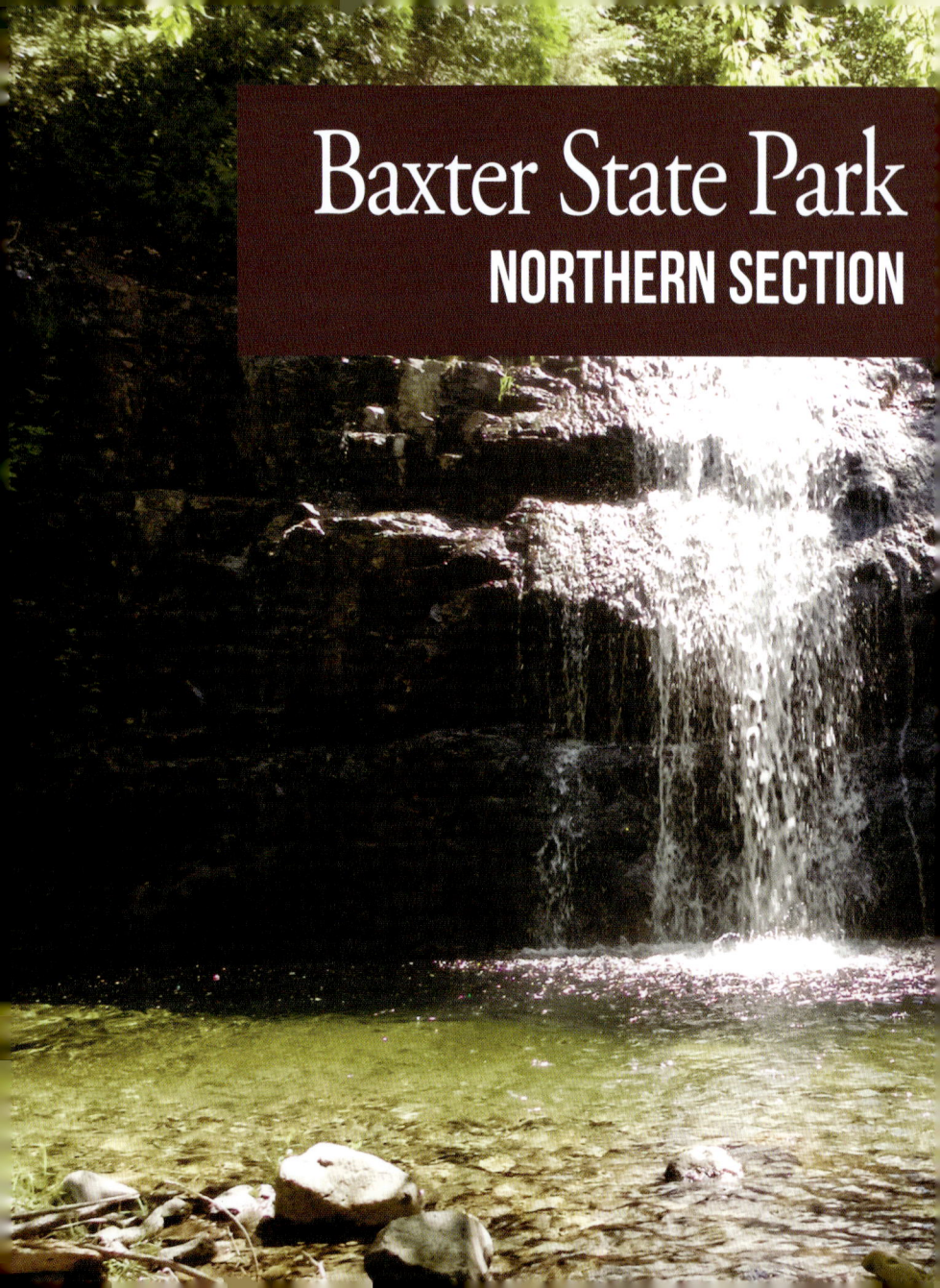

Baxter State Park
NORTHERN SECTION

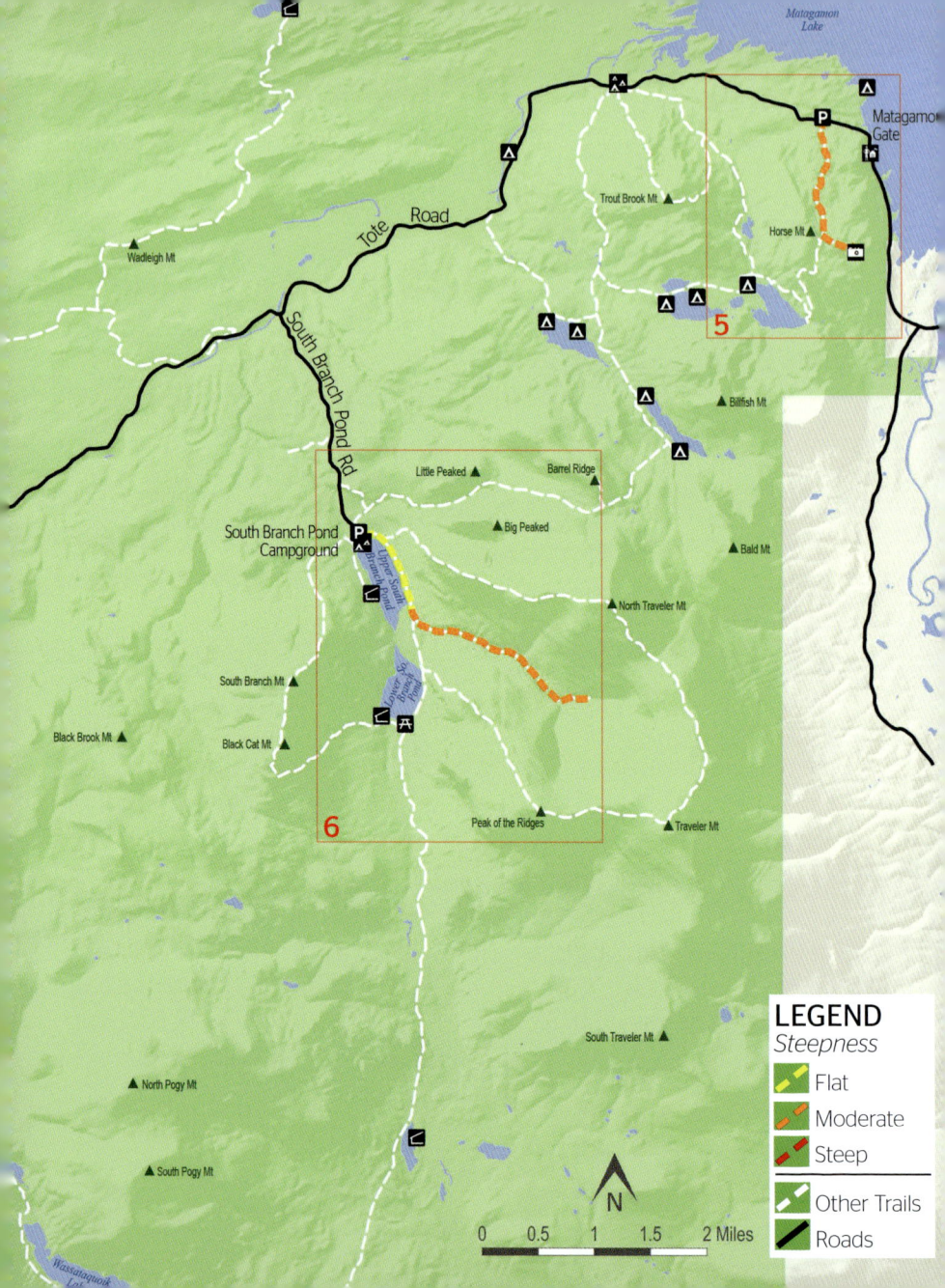

The northern part of Baxter State Park is accessed through Matagamon Gate off Grand Lake Road. Because it does not include trails to Katahdin and it is a little farther off the beaten path, it is less visited than the southern half, making it entirely possible for you to hike a trail and never see any other hikers along the way. This part of the park includes a Scientific Forest Management Area in its northwest corner—land that is managed for timber harvest and research, and in which hunting and trapping are allowed. (Hunting and trapping are not allowed in the rest of the park.)

For car camping, there are two campgrounds near Matagamon Gate (Trout Brook and South Branch Pond), and one campground (Nesowadnehunk Stream) halfway along the Tote Road between the north and south ends. The Tote Road will take you from the south part of the park to the north, but with a 20 mph speed limit along a narrow and twisty dirt road, it takes more than two hours. It's a long drive, but very pretty, and we saw some cool things along the way when we drove from Abol Campground up to South Branch Pond Campground.

We stopped at a place along Nesowadnehunk Stream called Ledge Falls. There were broad flat ledges here that were all worn smooth from the stream, creating natural water slides—a great place to swim! Gus and I had great fun here, while Mom and Dad ate lunch on the rocks and kept a close eye on us, making sure we stayed in the pools and out of the faster current, in case we took a tumble on the slippery rocks.

TRAILHEAD: From the Matagamon Gatehouse, drive 0.6 on the Tote Road to the small parking area and trailhead on the left.

DAY FIVE
Horse Mountain

Total Distance
2.8 miles

Difficulty
Moderate

Highest Elevation
1,589 feet

Time
2 to 2.5 hours

Bathrooms
None

Our hike today was filled with fabulous ferns and flowers! We went up the Horse Mountain Trail, which was mostly through trees but opened up to some views at an overlook.

The trail started by heading very gradually uphill through the forest. Everything was so green, with sunlight filtering through. There were birch trees and maple trees reaching up above us, and ferns, grasses, and all kinds of wildflowers at our feet. I really liked a pretty three-petaled one, which Mom said was called trillium.

At some point along the way, I noticed I was breathing heavier and it was harder to talk with Gus and my parents. I realized the trail was headed up more steeply than it had at the start.

After about a half-hour, the forest changed from birches and maples—trees that drop

their leaves in the fall—to evergreen spruce trees. It was here that we came to a trail junction. The Horse Mountain Trail continued straight toward the Horse Mountain summit and some ponds. A ranger had told us that the East Spur Overlook was actually nicer than the summit, so we skipped the summit itself and took a left to go to the overlook.

I was surprised when we started going downhill, and really steeply, too! But that didn't last long. The trail took us over a short rocky section, and then up to the rocky outcropping of the overlook. There were little spruces and other trees scattered around the pointed rocky ledges. We had to keep a sharp eye out for the blue paint marks on the rocks that led us to the best spot of the overlook.

From there, we could see some cliffs in front of us, part of Matagamon Lake below, and some low mountains and hills far in the distance. We also spotted some of the funniest-looking birds I've ever seen: turkey vultures. We found out later, from a ranger, that they have been nesting on the cliff faces of Horse Mountain in recent years. It was cool watching them soar through the air in front of us. They didn't even have to flap their wings, but just kept them outstretched and rode the currents in the wind. I wish I could fly and soar among the mountains like that.

After eating some apples and granola bars, Gus and I played hide-and-seek. All the little trees among the rocks and crevasses were perfect for it. Then we returned to the parking area, going down the same trail we had come up on.

FIELD NOTES

Turkey vultures are sometimes called buzzards. Their wingspan—the distance from the tip of one wing to the tip of the other, when the wings are stretched out—can be seven feet long! They eat carrion—recently dead animals. Yuck! Unusual for birds, they locate the decaying meat by smell.

EXTRAS: We followed a 0.8-mile self-guided nature trail in the Scientific Forest Management Area. It was an easy and fun way to learn about forestry and the SFMA. Named the Forestry Interpretive Trail, it begins about a half-mile down the Tote Road, heading west from the South Branch Pond Road. Brochures, which we picked up at the trailhead, guided us along the trail, and signs hung at kid-level—just right for Gus—told us the names of the different kinds of trees. It's a great add-on at the end of the day if you aren't ready to go back to your campsite yet, or a nice introductory hike on the day of your arrival.

Day Five: Horse Mountain

FIELD NOTES

Trillium are flowers named for their three petals, which come in several different colors. Their seeds have fleshy bits that ants like to collect to feed to their offspring. This helps the trillium spread and grow in new places.

NOTES

TRAILHEAD: From the Matagamon Gatehouse, drive 7 miles on the Tote Road. Take a left onto South Branch Pond Road and drive 2.2 miles to South Branch Pond Campground at the end of the road. There is a parking lot just before the campground entrance. You'll need to walk through the campground to get to the trailhead.

DAY SIX
Howe Brook

Total Distance
5.8 miles to Upper Falls
2.5 miles if you just go to the Lower Falls and back

Difficulty
Moderate to the Lower Falls; challenging sections along the trail to the Upper Falls

Highest Elevation
1,650 feet

Time
3 to 4 hours

Bathrooms
Yes
Outhouses at South Branch Pond Campground

I woke up this morning in our lean-to at South Branch Pond Campground to the sound of the water lapping at the shore. But then I heard something else. A critter scrambling through the brush? We peeked out, too late to catch sight of it. But when we looked at its tracks, I could tell it was a raccoon! I was glad our food was stashed safely in our car.

It was already really hot, and I knew it was going to get hotter. So I had my doubts when my dad announced it was time for a hike. Gus told him it was too hot, and I wholeheartedly agreed. "Ah, but it all depends on where you hike," my dad said, trying to convince us. It turns out he was right.

From South Branch Pond, we found the sign for the Pogy Notch Trail (which would take us to the Howe Brook Trail), at the corner of the dirt road that loops

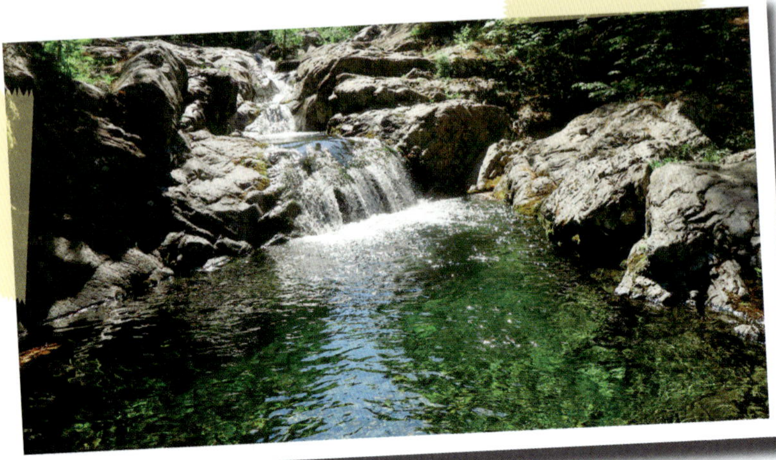

POCY NOTCH TRAIL
UPPER SO. BRANCH POND 0.4m →
JCT. CENTER RIDGE TRAIL 0.5 →
RUSSELL PD. CAMPGROUND 8.5 →
HOWE BROOK TRAIL
FALLS AND POOLS 0.2m. →
UPPER FALLS 2.0 →
B.S.P.
POCY NOTCH TRAIL
SOUTH BRANCH POND
CAMPGROUND
← 1.0m

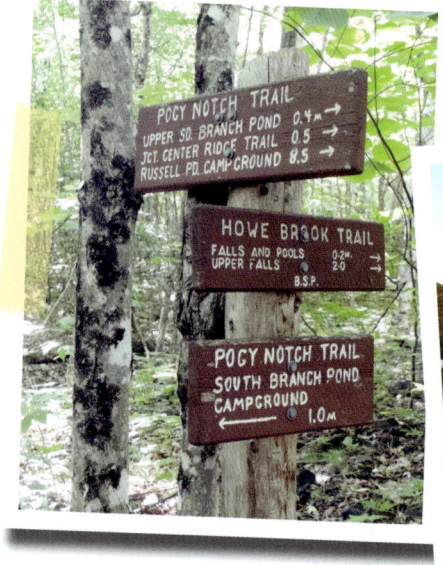

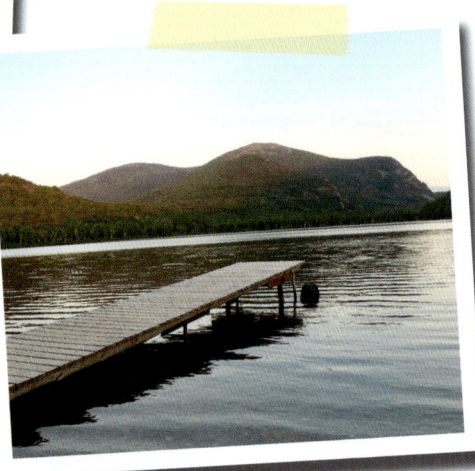

around the campground. It was just past the seven lean-tos dotted along the pond's edge. There was an intersection almost as soon as we set out. A trail branched off to the left, heading up North Traveler Mountain; we stayed to the right, taking the Pogy Notch Trail that follows the shore of the pond. It was pretty easy going, with boardwalks taking us over wet grassy areas at the beginning.

In under a half-hour, we came to Howe Brook on our right. There was a junction; the Pogy Notch Trail crossed over the brook to the right, but we went left, on the Howe Brook Trail. The trail followed the brook, and after just a few minutes, we came upon a waterfall with a giant pool below it. I immediately wanted to jump in the water, it looked so refreshing. Mom said we should swim *after* our hike, so after pausing a bit, we continued on. That was not the only pool; as we followed the brook, we passed many more small waterfalls and lots of little pools.

The brook then turned back into a more typical brook, with the water tumbling over lots of little boulders. The trail mostly followed alongside it, but in a couple of places, we had to climb steeply up a bank with the brook far below us, and then brace ourselves going back down the bank. In other places, we crossed over spots where the bank had eroded away. It was a little tricky, but we managed it.

We were in the woods, which shaded us from the sun, but it was still pretty hot out. I was glad when I heard a rushing of water that sounded like it could be the Upper Falls. False alarm! It was a different, smaller set of waterfalls that we could barely see, because the trail had strayed away from the brook at this point. But I still took it as a good sign that the Upper Falls were close, and I was right. There was a steep climb as we neared the falls, and then the trail bent to the right to take us right back to the brook—and there they were!

There was a huge, wide cliff face with water plunging right down the middle of it, and an inviting pool at the bottom. Mom and Dad suggested we save swimming for the deeper pools at the Lower Falls, though they let us wade around in this pool to cool down. The small rocks under my feet were a little rough and I almost fell, but I didn't care, the water felt so good.

After wading, and having water and snacks, we reluctantly re-booted our feet and headed back down the trail. On the way down, we stopped at the first set of the lower pools, nicely shaded by red spruce and white pine trees. We had come prepared, wearing our bathing suits under our clothes. I quickly discarded shoes, socks, shorts, and shirt, and jumped into the water. It was sooooo cold! I didn't stay in very long. But it felt so good on a hot day, I immediately jumped back in again! When I got out of the water, my skin felt all tingly. While I jumped in and out of the water, Gus and my dad found a smaller waterfall to sit under, the water splashing down right on top of their heads.

We spent the rest of the afternoon playing in the water and picnicking on the big rocks surrounding the pools before returning back, along the same trail, to the campground. What a great way to spend a hot day!

FIELD NOTES

Raccoons are medium-sized mammals that can live anywhere, from city streets, to rain forests, to the Maine woods. And they will eat anything! They particularly seem to like marshmallows that are left out by unsuspecting campers. Raccoons have an extremely sensitive sense of touch, and are quite intelligent, which makes them really good at opening zippers and locks.

FIELD NOTES

Red spruce trees are very straight, tall coniferous trees. They have short, yellow-green, pointed needles. If you look closely at them, you can see the needles have four sides. The bark is pretty cool-looking; it's a dark reddish-brown and is very scaly. Near the top of the Howe Brook Trail, there is a stand of virgin red spruce dating back more than 275 years.

NOTES

EXTRAS: If you want a break from hiking, you can still enjoy the Lower Falls of Howe Brook. Rent a canoe at South Branch Pond Campground, paddle down the pond about a mile to a canoe landing on the east side of the lake, and you'll only have to hike about a quarter of a mile from there to the Lower Falls! There were kids swimming off the dock at the campground; that looked like lots of fun, too, but we'd had enough swimming after our day in the waterfalls.

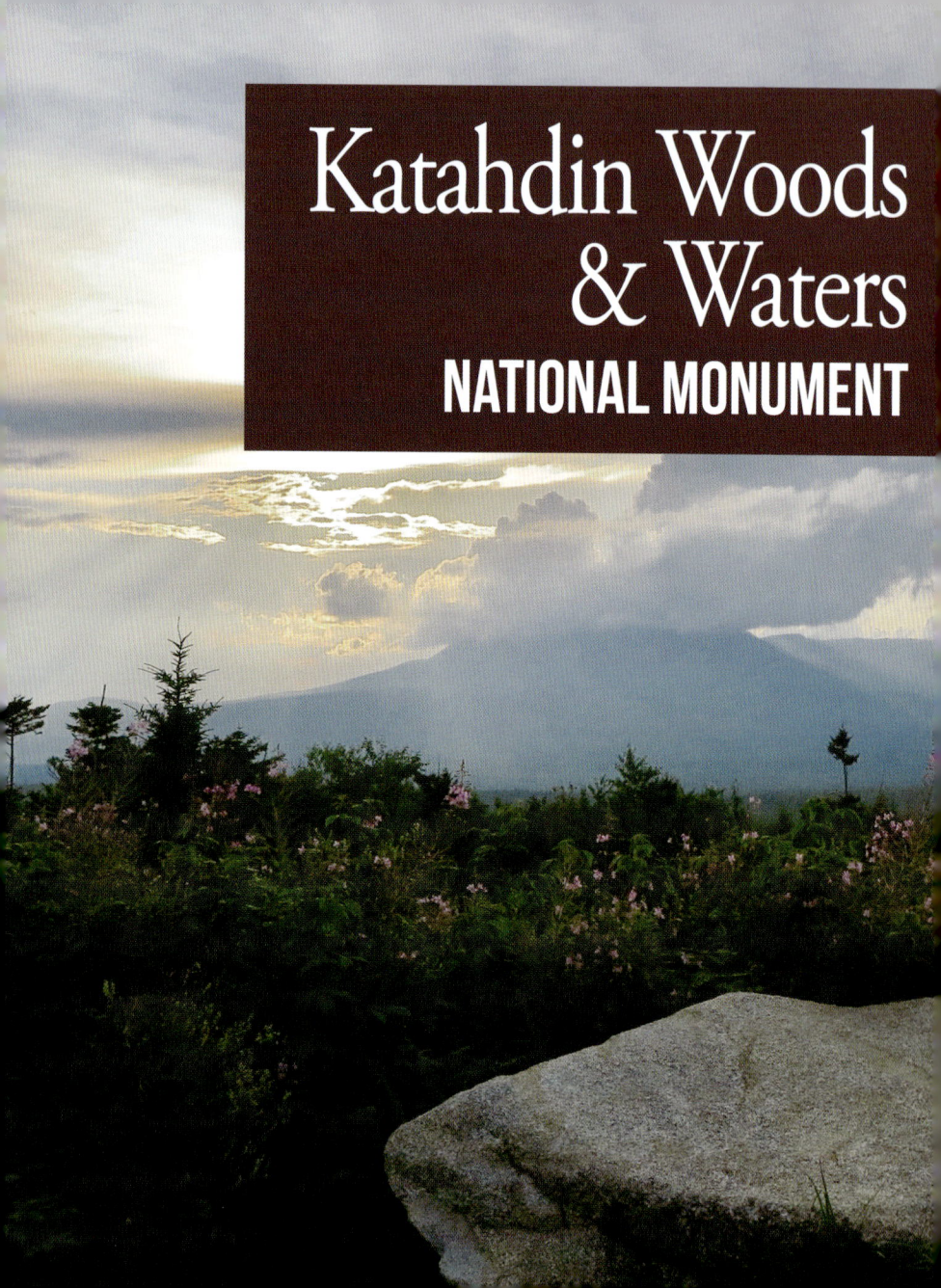

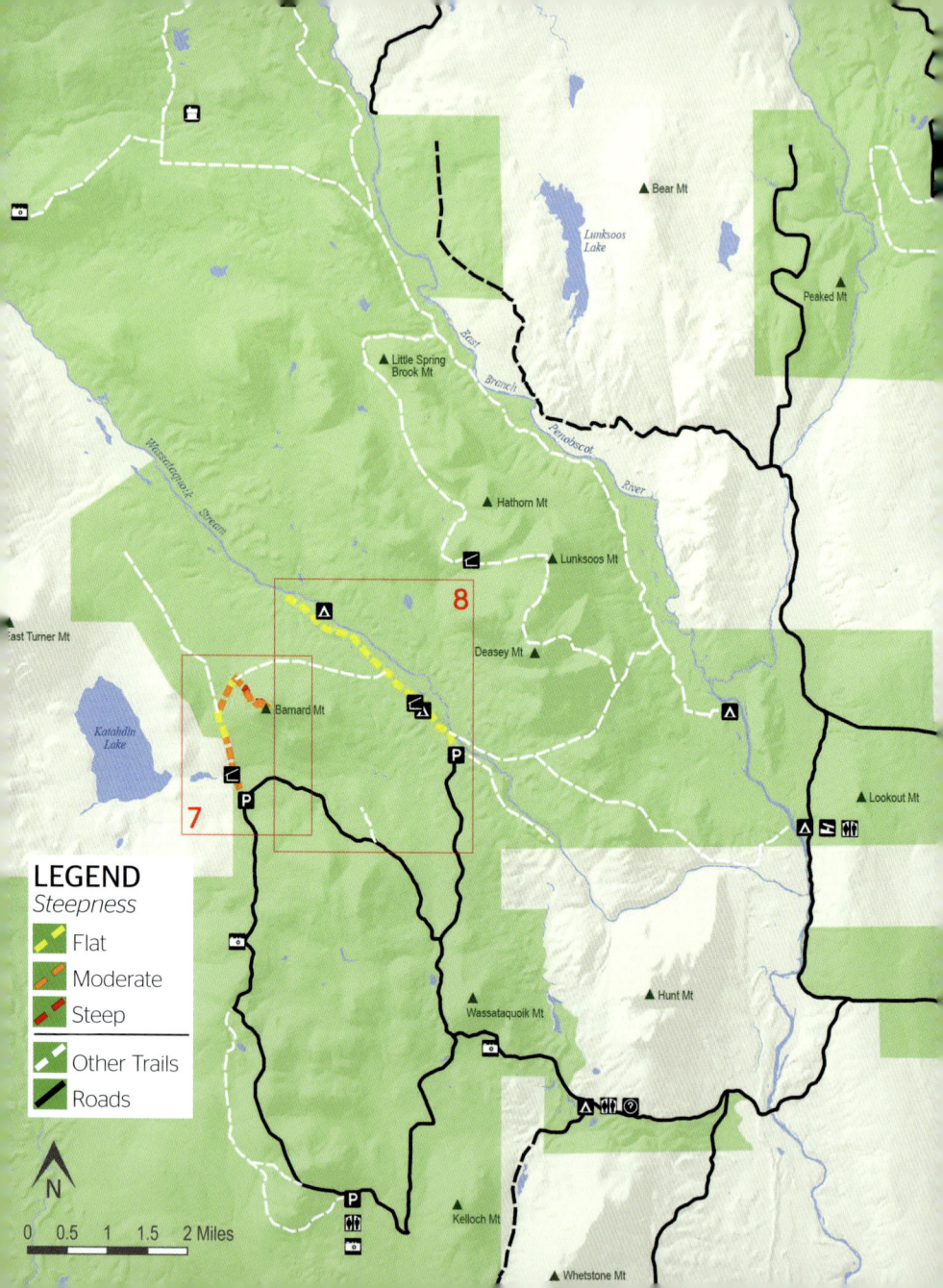

Katahdin Woods and Waters National Monument is made up of several large parcels of land in Penobscot County. Because it has only been a National Monument since 2016, it does not offer all the comforts you might find in some other national parks. What it *does* offer is unspoiled rivers and streams, habitat for rare wildlife, and plenty of recreational opportunities for hikers, campers, and boaters. The 16-mile gravel loop road through the southern section of the area is well marked, has two scenic vistas with amazing views of Katahdin, and offers opportunities for hiking along the way.

In addition to various lean-tos for backpackers scattered throughout the area, car camping is available at Sandbank Stream, on a first-come, first-served basis. The Katahdin Brook lean-to is a good camping option; it's away from the loop road, but not too far away! This is where I stayed with my family. The lean-to is about a quarter of a mile from the parking area, where you can also find the trailhead for the Barnard Mountain hike. It's marked by an International Appalachian Trail/Barnard Mountain trail sign. We had to carry all of our gear in, and it also meant we—okay, mainly Dad—had to carry our food back to the car that distance for the night, or else hang it in a bag from a tree, so that bears and smaller critters couldn't steal it! But it was totally worth this little bit of extra effort to stay there near the brook. Because this lean-to is on the International Appalachian Trail, if an IAT hiker had stopped here for the night, we would have had a lean-to-mate, but we had it to ourselves while we were there.

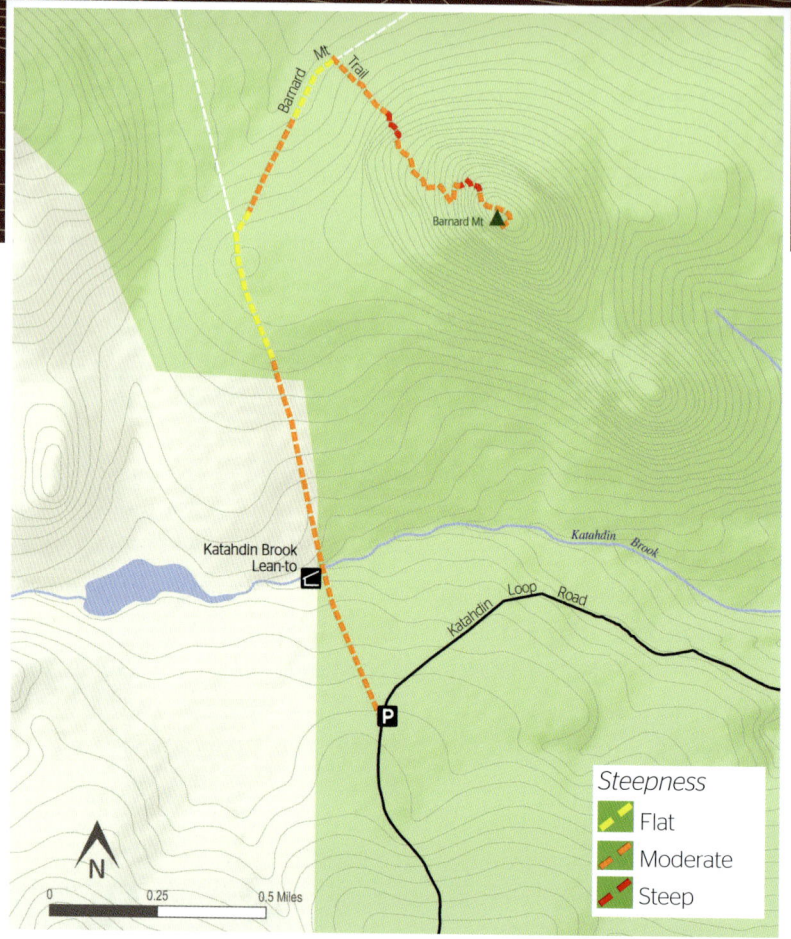

TRAILHEAD: Take Swift Brook Road from Route 11 in Stacyville. In about 5 miles, veer left at the fork. You'll pass Sandbank Stream campsite about 5 miles later, and shortly after, you'll see a sign at a gate for Katahdin Woods and Waters National Monument. In another 2 miles, you will reach the Katahdin Loop Road. Turn right to travel counterclockwise around the loop. In approximately 5 miles, take the pull-off on the right and park there. You will see the trailhead indicating Barnard Mountain and the International Appalachian Trail (IAT); this trail leads to the Katahdin Brook lean-to as well.

DAY SEVEN
Barnard Mountain

Total Distance
4.6 Miles

Difficulty
Easy; moderate on the path in the woods up to the summit

Highest Elevation
1,621 feet

Time
2 to 2.5 hours

Bathrooms
None

I wasn't so sure about today's hike when I looked down the trail continuing off to the left from the Katahdin Brook lean-to. Like the first short part of this trail we had taken, to get from the parking area to the lean-to, it seemed more like a narrow dirt road, and it rose straight and steep into the distance. It was quite hot and humid, too, which was making Gus grumpy. But we had set out to hike Barnard Mountain, so hiking Barnard Mountain is what we were going to do!

It turned out that the road-like trail wasn't as steep as it had seemed. There were tons of wildflowers growing along the trailside. I took lots of pictures of them, so I could look them up and identify them later. There were some raspberries growing there, too, which we picked and munched on along the way. I love it when the trail provides food for us!

Not long after getting to the top of a hill, we followed a sign to Barnard Mountain on a trail branching off to the right. This was similar to the first stretch, but the dirt road was a little narrower. It led us gently downward, which was a bit of a relief.

The next trail junction was also well marked, with a sign to the Barnard Mountain summit pointing us to a woodsy path on the right. We started heading back up, though not too steeply, on this path over dirt and leaves, through a forest of mostly beech trees.

We weren't among the trees for long, when, all of a sudden, I heard a *wump-wump-wump* right in front of us. I caught a quick glimpse of a fat brown bird flying off. Its flapping wings had made that noise! It landed back on the ground just down the trail. Dad said it was a spruce grouse. It blended in really well with the trees and the leaves on the ground.

We then came to a giant boulder, and at first, I couldn't figure out where the trail went; the path seemed to go right *through* the boulder! It actually went between the big boulder and another slightly smaller one right next to it. They looked like they may have started out as one rock that got broken in two. There was just barely enough space for us to walk through, single file.

The woods turned into mostly spruce trees and the trail flattened out, so I figured we were getting near the summit. Sure enough, we came around a bend to see rocks, placed as steps, leading up to a big, broad ledge, and an opening in the trees ahead. A picnic table was perched at the edge of the ledge, with amazing views west over Katahdin Lake, to Katahdin itself, and all the

mountains of Baxter State Park. I was glad we had brought our lunch, so we could sit and eat and enjoy this spot for a while.

I could have stayed there all afternoon, but Gus was getting antsy, and my parents kept eyeing the storm clouds that were floating around the top of Katahdin. So down we went, back the same way we had come.

Near the end of the Barnard Mountain trail, we passed by the Katahdin Brook lean-to where we were staying and continued just a bit farther, to cool off at Katahdin Brook. There was a bridge across this small brook, and although there were no pools deep enough for swimming, there was enough water to sit and let the water rush swiftly around me.

After the hike, playing in the brook, and getting into dry clothes in the lean-to, all of a sudden there was a flash of light, then *KABOOM!* The thunderstorms that had been threatening all day had finally reached us. I was glad we were under shelter, because a slow tapping of rain soon turned into a heavy downpour! I love a good storm. It was fun being able to enjoy it while staying dry and safe in the lean-to, particularly after a great hike.

FIELD NOTES

The **raspberries** you'll find growing in Maine are usually of the red variety, but sometimes you may find black ones as well. Each individual raspberry consists of about a hundred individual tiny fruits, called drupelets, and each drupelet contains one single seed.

FIELD NOTES

Spruce grouse waddle around on the ground in the summer, eating pine and spruce needles. They like to live in cold northern climates, and Maine is about as far south as you'll find them. They can be hard to see because they are well camouflaged, but if you hear a rustling on the ground along the trail, keep your eyes peeled—you might just see one.

NOTES

EXTRAS: The 16-mile Loop Road is a must-do here. There is a lookout and picnic area about 4.5 miles around the loop, if you're traveling clockwise from Swift Brook Road, which has a nice view of Katahdin. There are two cool signs with profiles of all the mountains you are looking at, etched in wood, with their names. There were a couple of other viewpoints along the way, too, and we read some interesting things in an interpretive map we had picked up from the kiosk at Sandbank Stream on our way in. We did the loop after dinner, which was perfect timing, as the sun was just about to go down behind Katahdin.

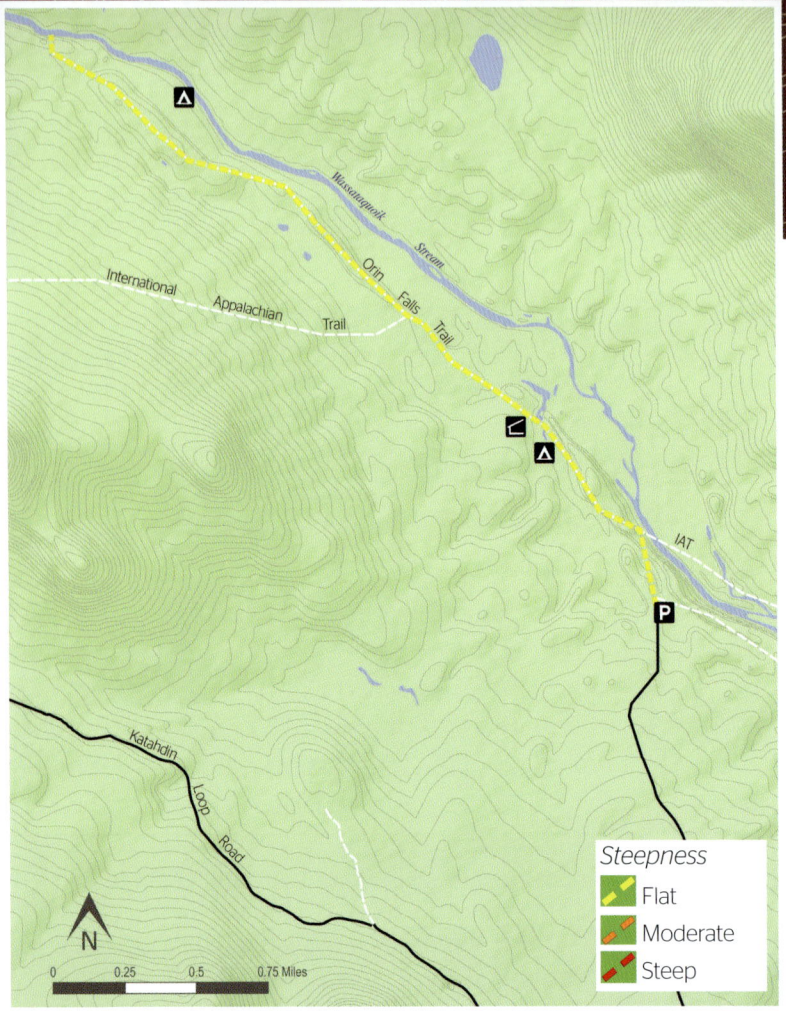

TRAILHEAD: Take Swift Brook Road from Route 11 in Stacyville. In about 5 miles, veer left at the fork. You'll pass Sandbank Stream campsite about 5 miles later. In another 2 miles, you will reach the Katahdin Loop Road, turn right. In 1.3 miles, take a right onto Orin Falls Road. Travel 2.5 miles to the end of this bumpy dirt road to the trailhead.

DAY EIGHT
Orin Falls

Total Distance
5.8 Miles

Difficulty
Easy

Highest Elevation
720 feet

Time
2.5 to 3 hours

Bathrooms
None

After hiking a mountain yesterday, we were happy to take a mostly flat trail along the Wassataquoik Stream today. Plus, it was a thunderstorm-y day, raining off and on, with lots of fog banks floating around the mountains, so there might not have been much to see from a mountain summit anyway.

Our destination: waterfalls! At the trailhead, there was a sign to the falls, as well as a sign to Barnard Mountain (the mountain we hiked yesterday). This is a different way to get up Barnard—a route twice as long as the one we had taken.

We headed off on a gravel track. There were a couple of paths that broke off to the right, but we continued straight ahead on the main track. I knew from looking at the map that the stream was to our right, but we couldn't really see it. The trail here is part of the International Appalachian Trail, or IAT, which extends the AT from Mount Katahdin into Canada.

After about a half-hour, we crossed a rotting bridge over a brook and came upon a campsite on the left. There was a lean-to and also a place to put a tent. It looked like a nice place to camp if you don't mind carrying all your gear this far! Just past it, the track got much grassier. Ruts on either side provided a place to walk, and tall grasses, wildflowers, and baby trees were growing down the center.

I heard a crashing sound through the woods, and a breathy noise I couldn't identify. Then Gus heard it, and then Mom and Dad heard it, too. We stopped to look more closely, and I saw a large, dark shape through the trees. It was a bear! I couldn't believe I was seeing a bear! It was pretty far away, and as cool as it was to see it, I was sort of glad it wasn't closer. We didn't linger, but quickly proceeded on the trail, *away* from the bear!

At the next trail junction, the IAT headed off to the left, and we continued straight. The sign said it was another 1.56 miles to Orin Falls. We were halfway there! A good thing, too, because I was so hungry that I was sure my stomach was growling loud enough to scare away any wildlife.

Just when I thought I couldn't bear it anymore, I heard the sound of rushing water. Could it be the falls? Nope. It was just a small brook we crossed over, on a bridge. But just around the corner, we came to a sign pointing us to the right, toward Orin Falls. As we came to the end of this path, cinnamon ferns and

Day Eight: Orin Falls

cedar trees framed our view of Orin Falls and the Wassataquoik Stream. It wasn't a waterfall like some of the others we had seen, where one big sheet of water spills down over a cliff. Instead, there were giant boulders everywhere in the stream, and the water found its way around or over them. The currents and cascades and tumbling water were too strong for us to play in, but we did wade in some of the small pools off to the side.

After getting some food in my belly, cooling off my feet, and enjoying the amazing falls, I felt ready for the long trek back, the same way we had come. We kept Gus happy by playing some rounds of "I Spy" and "Twenty Questions" as we walked.

EXTRAS: Not far from the trailhead, as you begin this hike, there is a trail on the right that leads down to, and across, the Wassataquoik Stream. It is a part of the International Appalachian Trail. If you are willing to brace yourself to ford the stream through knee- to thigh-deep water (I probably could have done it, but Gus would have needed a piggyback ride across), it continues on a narrow path through the woods, along the banks of the stream on the other side.

FIELD NOTES

Black bears are small compared to other bears and are the only kind of bears in Maine. There are more of them here than in any other state besides Alaska. In spite of their numbers, you aren't all that likely to see one, as they live in large tracts of wild spaces and are rather shy, avoiding people whenever possible. However, make sure you store your food properly while camping as it could attract a bear's attention.

FIELD NOTES

Cinnamon fern grows in moist, wet areas, such as in swamps or around the edges of ponds. The ferns don't produce cinnamon, or even smell like cinnamon; they were named for the color of their shorter fronds. Cinnamon ferns have been around for 180 million years!

NOTES

Debsconeag Lakes
WILDERNESS AREA

The Debsconeag Lakes Wilderness Area, or DLWA, covers more than 46,000 acres of land—that's so big, you could almost fit two Disney Worlds in there!—and is owned by The Nature Conservancy. It has been protected as an ecological reserve since 2002. An ecological reserve is land that has been set aside for conservation and for studying the biological communities—the plants and animals—that live there and to see how they interact with each other and the physical environment.

Debsconeag means "Carrying Place." The Native people of the area gave it this name because it contains many portages—trails over which they had to carry their canoes between ponds. This wilderness area contains pockets of old-growth hemlock forest, which means no trees in the area have ever been cut down by people or destroyed by nature.

There are some backcountry campsites within the DLWA; many are free, on a first-come, first-served basis, and you have to carry in (and carry out) all your gear. There are also a few state-owned campgrounds as well as private campgrounds nearby, if car camping is more your style.

We camped at the Horserace Brook camping area, one of the state-owned campgrounds, at a tent site that had a view of Katahdin. It was about five miles farther down the Golden Road from the Abol Bridge Store, but just before the road to the Horserace Pond trailhead. At some of the other camping areas directly on the Golden Road, you could hear trucks going by, but this one was pretty quiet. There is a boat launch here, too; I wish we had brought a canoe with us.

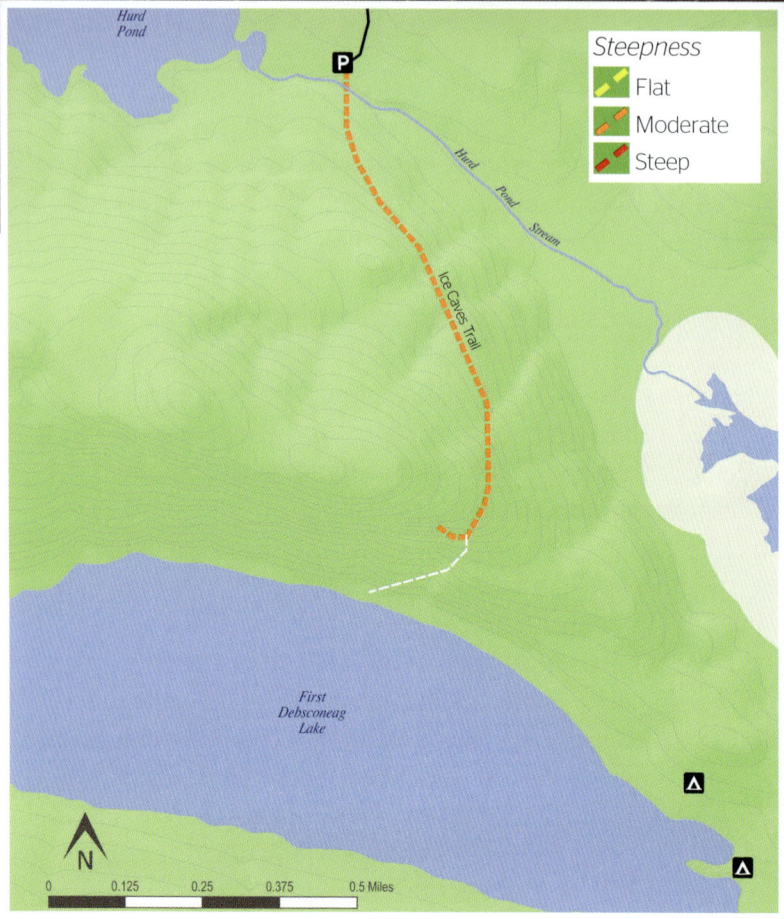

TRAILHEAD: From Millinocket, follow the signs for Baxter State Park, taking a right onto Katahdin Avenue from Route 11/157, and at the next intersection with Bates Street, bearing left. Follow Millinocket Road (the Baxter State Park Road) for about 8 miles. Just after the North Woods Trading Post general store, take a left onto a short spur road that will take you to the Golden Road, and turn right. The Golden Road is partially paved and it can be quite bumpy. You will reach the Abol Bridge Campground after 10 miles. Cross Abol Bridge and turn onto the well-marked road on the left. The trailhead is at the end of this 3.3-mile dirt road, which is very bumpy and overgrown in places.

DAY NINE
Ice Caves

Total Distance
2 miles

Difficulty
Moderate

Highest Elevation
800 feet

Time
1 to 2 hours

Bathrooms
Yes
Outhouse located shortly down the road from the parking area

Yes, there really is *ice*, lots of it, in the middle of summer! It was so cool! But I'm getting ahead of myself...

It was pretty cloudy when I stuck my head out of the tent this morning and looked out across the Penobscot River—and cold! So, it seemed appropriate to visit a place called the ice caves.

After a bumpy car ride, we came to a small parking area and a big red gate across the road, keeping us from driving any farther. On the other side of the gate was a wide wooden bridge. We parked, then walked across the bridge onto a broad gravel track. Almost immediately, there was a sign to our left pointing to a path through the woods for the ice caves and First Debsconeag Lake.

This trail took us through an otherworldly forest of tall spruce trees. I say otherworldly because it felt like we were in the land of giants. Scattered through the woods were humongous boulders, most of them way too big to climb. They were covered in moss and had lots of feathery ferns growing all over them. On the ground between the boulders, I spotted the strangest-looking white plants; I later identified them in my field guide as Indian pipe. Gus kept running ahead of us, hiding behind a boulder, and jumping out from behind it to say "Boo!"

I loved everything about this trail! We continued on through the spruces and boulders, with some uphills but no big climbs. Eventually, we started going downhill, and came to a trail sign. To the right was a scenic vista; to the left were the ice caves. We decided to go check out the vista first. Because it was a drizzly day, we could not see much more than the lake right below us. Everything else was shrouded in fog. After returning to the main trail, we then came to another sign. The ice caves were to the right and Debsconeag Lake was to the left. We headed to the right and almost immediately came upon the caves.

At first, I saw only a metal railing and some metal steps amid some boulders and rocky ledges. Then I realized they were leading down into a hole! It was a bit scary, peering down into that deep, dark hole with the metal rungs disappearing downward. I could see some ice near the top. It was strange to see ice in the middle of summer! There wasn't a lot of space at the bottom of the ladder, so first Dad helped Gus down, and after they came back up, I went down with Mom.

Photo by Wendy Almeida

It was a bit tricky getting down, because the bottom rungs were covered in ice, so Mom had to help me at the bottom. The cave went down much farther, but we stayed on a small shelf near the bottom of the ladder and took it all in. Long sheets of ice covered the cave walls. There was ice in the cracks of rock, and chunks of ice scattered on the cave floor. I had thought the giant boulders in the woods were otherworldly, but in this cave, I really felt like we were on another planet. It was so different from anything else I had ever experienced!

If you want to descend to the bottom of the cave, make sure you bring crampons or some other kind of traction for your feet. You'll want to bring a headlamp, too, and gloves and warm clothes, if you want to spend more than a few minutes exploring. It was so cold, I could even see my breath!

It was weird, but nice, to come back out into a summer day. As I came up the ladder, I heard a haunting *who-cooks-for-you* call coming from the trees. I knew right away that it was a barred owl! I had thought owls only come out at night, but it turns out some owls will hunt and occasionally call during the daytime, and the barred owl is more likely to do so on a cloudy day. The owl continued to call as we made our way back through the spruce and boulder landscape, keeping us company as we returned to the trailhead.

FIELD NOTES

Barred owls get their name from the pattern of white and brown bars on their feathers. While most owls have yellow eyes, the barred owl has brown eyes. They like to eat small rodents, such as mice and moles. They swallow them whole, then regurgitate the bones and fur, and anything else they can't digest, in a pellet. If you're lucky enough to find an owl pellet, pull it apart and see what you can find!

FIELD NOTES

Indian pipe is entirely white, which gives this wildflower an unusual and ghostly look. Green plants get energy from the sun, but the Indian pipe gets its energy from a fungus, which in turn gets its energy from trees. Pretty cool! Since it doesn't need sunlight, it can grow in very dark environments, such as the understory of a dense forest.

NOTES

EXTRAS: The sun came out and the afternoon was as warm as the morning was cold, so we took a break from hiking and went tubing down the Penobscot River. From the Abol Bridge Campground and Store, we picked up tubes and took a shuttle bus upriver. We drifted our way down the river back to Abol Bridge, lazily floating along in our tubes and playing in the water.

TRAILHEAD: From Millinocket, follow the signs for Baxter State Park, taking a right onto Katahdin Avenue from Route 11/157, and at the next intersection with Bates Street, bearing left. Follow Millinocket Road (the Baxter State Park Road) for about 8 miles. Just after the North Woods Trading Post general store, take a left onto a short spur road that will take you to the Golden Road, and turn right. The Golden Road is partially paved, but quite bumpy and slow-going. You will reach the Abol Bridge Campground after 10 miles. Cross Abol Bridge and continue for 5 miles. Just after the sign for Horserace Brook camping area, there's a road on the left; take this dirt road about a quarter of a mile to the end, and park in the small lot.

DAY TEN
Horserace Loop

Total Distance
6 miles

Parking Lot to Horserace Pond (on the Yellow Trail): 1.9 miles

Horserace Pond to summit (on the Orange Trail): 1.2 miles

Summit to intersection with Blue Trail (on the Orange Trail): 1.3 miles

Intersection to parking lot (on the Blue and Yellow Trails): 1.6 miles

Difficulty
Challenging

Highest Elevation
1,670 feet

Time
4 to 5 hours

Bathrooms
None

The Horserace Loop was our hike of the day today, the last one of our trip! It was a long hike, but worth the effort. At the well-marked trailhead, we crossed a bridge and followed a short spur trail before getting to the loop itself. At the trail junction, we headed to the right to do the loop in a counterclockwise direction.

I thought I heard a breeze picking up, which would have been great, because this section of trail was *really* buggy! But I learned that wind blowing through the trees and the rush of water over stones can sound the same; what I was actually hearing was Horserace Brook. We walked with the brook on our right for a while, climbing higher along the rocky trail.

After hiking for a little over an hour, we came to Horserace Pond. There were a couple of campsites on the hill looking down on the pond. It would be so cool to camp there! But maybe not so cool to have to carry in a tent, sleeping bag, clothes, food, supplies . . .

We followed the shore of the pond for just a short time before coming to the next signpost. There was no trail junction, but the sign said that it was 1.2 miles to the summit, on the Orange Trail. As we left the banks of the pond, we really started going uphill in earnest. It was quite the climb!

On the way up, we passed through an area of old-growth hemlock trees, which means no trees in the area have *ever* been cut down by people or destroyed by nature, so some of the trees are very big. I really liked these groves. It was shady but open underneath, with no brush or bushes to walk through, and soft needles under our feet.

Past these groves, the trail became sunnier, and instead of following a path, we were hiking on rocky ledges. Before we knew it, we had reached the summit! There was no sign telling us it was the summit, but there were signs showing the distances back to the parking area in either direction, so we knew we were almost exactly halfway around the loop.

I could see all sorts of things from here. There was a big, long lake—Rainbow Lake—below us; there was a ridge of mountains in the distance; and to the northeast, off to the left, in the direction the trail continued, I could see Katahdin peeking from behind the trees. The summit was a great spot for lunch, so we hung out there for a while, and I got to feed my hungry stomach and rest my weary legs.

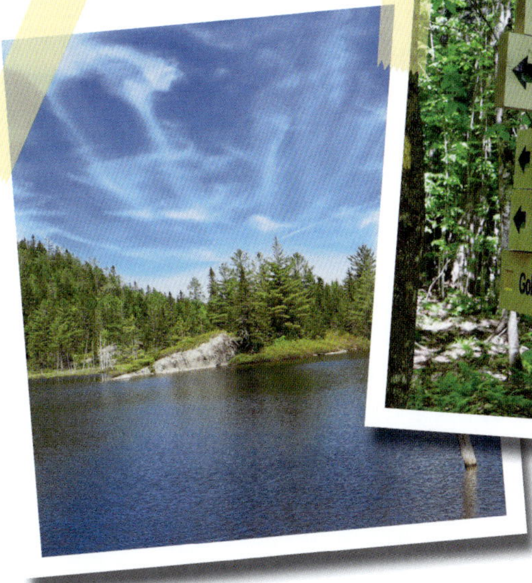

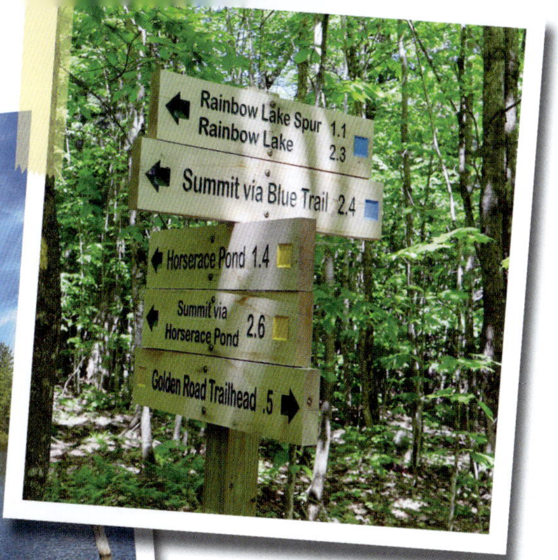

Rainbow Lake Spur 1.1
Rainbow Lake 2.3
Summit via Blue Trail 2.4
Horserace Pond 1.4
Summit via
Horserace Pond 2.6
Golden Road Trailhead .5

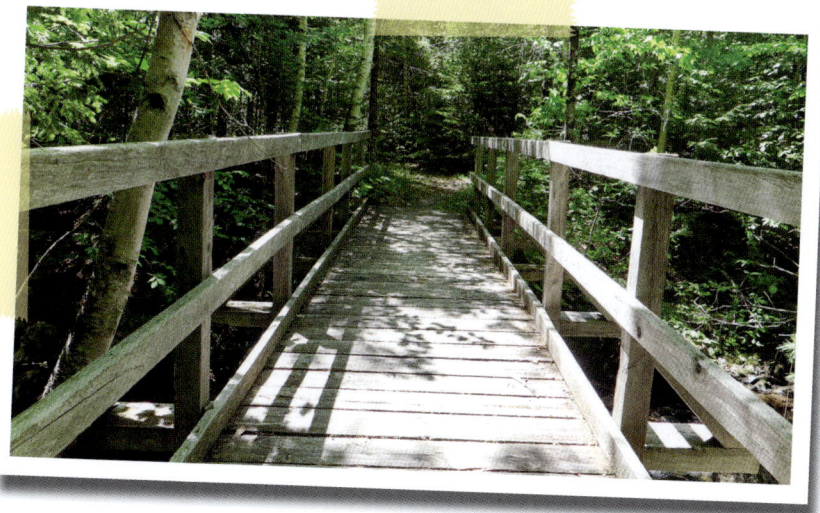

After lunch, we followed the trail along rocky ledges, with lichen and blueberry bushes and mountain laurel at our feet. We also passed a small marshy pond. Gus wanted to stop here to look for frogs, but our parents made us keep going, because we still had a long way to go. We encountered a second pretty impressive vista—it felt like another summit!—before heading back down into the woods.

Once we were heading downhill, we moved a little faster, so it wasn't long before we came to the next trail junction. A father and son were just coming up the trail from the right, the trail to Rainbow Lake. They had been fishing and showed us the brook trout they had caught. The lake and trail sounded nice, but we did not want to add any more miles to our already lengthy hike. So, we went to the left to continue around the loop.

We were now on the Blue Trail. This section of the trail had quite a lot of downhills, too. As much as I was enjoying the hike—except for those pesky bugs—I wasn't entirely sad when I saw a trail junction with signs indicating we had completed the loop. We turned right and had only another half-mile along the spur trail back to our car. I was ready to rest, and was looking forward to a giant, hearty dinner!

It was a big hike, but worth the effort. It included so many different types of environments, reminding me of all the other amazing trails my family and I had hiked over the past ten days. It was great way to finish our trip to the North Woods!

FIELD NOTES

Brook trout are brownish-green fish that have a marbled pattern across their sides, and are found in freshwater lakes, ponds, and streams. They are more likely to be found in cold, clear, pure water. They have lots of nicknames, including mud trout, squaretail, speckled trout, brookie, baiser, lord fish, and slob.

FIELD NOTES

Hemlock trees are conifers (which means they have needles, not leaves) that can live a really long time, sometimes more than five hundred years. Their needles, which are full of lots of vitamin C, were used by Native Americans to make tea. These trees are important to the ecology of the forest. Their needles, bark, and seeds provide food for animals. They also provide shade for brooks and streams, keeping waters cool for trout and other cold-water species.

NOTES

EXTRAS: We stopped at Nesowadnehunk Falls, along the Golden Road, about 2 miles east of the road to the Horserace Loop trailhead, to see some impressive scenery. There's a view of Katahdin downstream, but also paddlers getting tossed around as they go through these falls on the Penobscot River. The falls are too dangerous for your average kayaker, but there were lots of whitewater rafters braving the rapids when we were there. It looked like scary fun. Next time!

Photo by Melissa Kim

The Essentials

BAXTER STATE PARK

Getting there: The park has two gatehouses—one in the south called Togue Pond, and one in the north called Matagamon. The south gatehouse is about 16 miles from Millinocket. The north gatehouse is about 35 miles from Patten.

Entrance fees/passes: Day use is free for Mainers; there is a $15 entrance fee for cars with non-Maine license plates. Some of the parking lots (the Katahdin trailheads Roaring Brook, Abol, and Katahdin Stream) require a $5 parking reservation for day hiking (full details here: baxterstatepark.org/general-info/#reserve).

Camping: There are many camping options within the park, including tent sites, lean-tos, bunkhouses, cabins, and group sites. There are campgrounds you can drive to, remote backcountry campgrounds, and individual backcountry sites. Summer camping fees range from $12 for a bed in a bunkhouse to $21 to $32 for a campsite, to $135 for a large cabin. Sites must be reserved well in advance; camping reservations are made on a rolling basis, and open up four months in advance. If you want to camp in August, make your reservation in April (by phone, mail, in person in Millinocket, or online: baxterstatepark.org/camp-summer/#reserve).

Roads: The Tote Road runs the length of the Park. Because the park's dirt roads are narrow and twisty, large vehicles such as RVs are prohibited.

Biking: Allowed on the Park Tote Road and the Dwelley Pond Trail, as well as on those portions of the Scientific Forest Management Area (SFMA) road system not in use for logging. Mountain biking is not permitted on the hiking trails.

Fires: Allowed in designated fire rings, but no firewood is allowed to be brought into the park.

Dogs: Not allowed.

Water: There is no potable water in the park. Bring your own! Also, it's pack-in, pack-out in the park.

Additional information:
baxterstatepark.org
Park Headquarters, 64 Balsam Drive, Millinocket
(207) 723-5140

Friends of Baxter State Park
friendsofbaxter.org

This independent organization offers a lot of very useful information and history about the park, as well as an events calendar, programs, trip planning advice, and more.

KATAHDIN WOODS AND WATERS NATIONAL MONUMENT

Getting there: There are currently two main access points. The south entrance and Katahdin Loop Road can be reached from Swift Brook Road. From Medway, take Route 11 for approximately 20 miles and look for the turn onto Swift Brook Road. This is a gravel road, shared with logging trucks. The North/Matagamon entrance is about 30 miles from the intersection of Route 11 and Route 159 in Patten.

Detailed directions: nps.gov/kaww/planyourvisit/directions.htm

Entrance fees/passes: Day use is free.

Camping: Lean-tos, tent sites, and two huts are available in the National Monument on a first-come, first-served basis. There is no camping fee. You must backpack in to most sites. You can reach Sandbank Stream, Lunksoos, and Upper East Branch camping areas by car.

Roads: The two entrance roads leading into, and the roads inside of, the Monument are all unpaved. A high-clearance vehicle is recommended for unimproved roads, but they are passable in a sedan if you drive slowly. RVs or trailers are not recommended. Roads can be narrow in some sections, so be prepared to pull aside for oncoming traffic. Logging trucks always have the right-of-way.

Biking: Mountain biking is currently permitted on the Monument gravel roads and trails. This could change as management plans develop; check the website for the latest information.

Fires: Allowed in designated locations, with a valid Maine Forest Service campfire permit (no fee).

Dogs: Allowed, if kept on a leash and kept out of the shelters and lean-tos.

Parking: Parking permits are required if you are going to park overnight, except if you are camping at the Sandbank Stream, Lunksoos, or Upper East Branch camping areas.

Additional information:
nps.gov/kaww
(207) 456-6001

Friends of Katahdin Woods and Waters
friendsofkww.org

The website for this nonprofit has a lot of useful information, including directions; nearby accommodations; suggested hiking, biking, and paddling trips; maps; and an online shop where you can order waterproof trail maps and an interpretive trail map.

DEBSCONEAG LAKES WILDERNESS AREA

Getting there: The Wilderness Area is most easily accessed via the Golden Road from Millinocket, from the north and east, or via an unimproved road through state land from the southwest.

Entrance fees/passes: Day use is free.

Camping: Within the DLWA itself, The Nature Conservancy owns several backcountry camping sites. There are no fees and no reservations, and it's strictly pack-in, pack-out. A couple of state-owned backcountry campgrounds are located nearby along the Golden Road, with sites available, on a first-come first-served basis, for a small fee ($6 for Maine residents; $12 for nonresidents; call 207-941-4014 for more information). These sites are considered river camping, and are part of the Penobscot River Corridor, Bureau of Parks and Lands.

Roads: The Golden Road is a pothole-riddled, mostly dirt road that is used primarily by logging trucks. There are just a couple of short unimproved dirt roads within the Wilderness Area itself; a vehicle with high clearance is recommended.

Biking: Mountain biking is not permitted on the hiking trails.

Fires: Allowed in designated locations, with a valid Maine Forest Service campfire permit (no fee).

Dogs: Not allowed.

Additional information:
The Nature Conservancy
nature.org/ourinitiatives/regions/northamerica/unitedstates/maine/placesweprotect/debsconeag-lakes-wilderness-area.xml

Helpful Resources

Katahdin Area Trails
katahdinareatrails.org

Katahdin Area Trails is a nonprofit dedicated to creating recreation trails that are both environmentally and economically sustainable, and purpose-built for hiking, skiing, or mountain biking. The website includes a trail finder.

Katahdin Chamber of Commerce
katahdinmaine.com

The Chamber of Commerce has a guide to activities, lodging, restaurants, and more in the greater Katahdin area.

Katahdin Woods and Waters Scenic Byway
katahdinwoodsandwaters.com

The 89-mile-long designated Scenic Byway goes from the southern edge of Baxter State Park toward Millinocket, along the Penobscot River, north to Patten, and ends at the northern entrance to Baxter State Park. The website offers information about things to see and do, profiles of local artists, resources, maps, photos, and videos.

Maine Youth Wilderness Leadership Program
friendsofbaxter.org/programs/mywlp

Maine high school sophomores and juniors are eligible to apply for this nine-day wilderness experience.

Millinocket Welcome Center
200 Penobscot Avenue, Millinocket

This welcome center for the Katahdin Woods and Waters National Monument has some basic information and orientation. It's open from June through early October from 8 a.m. till 4 p.m. From October through May, it is only open on Thursdays from 1 to 4 p.m.

Things To Do

MUSEUMS, LIBRARIES, AND MORE

The Ambajejus Boom House
themaineboomhouses.org

On Ambajejus Lake, this little island is home to the Ambajejus Boom House, a restored house where logging workers lived that preserves a piece of Maine's logging history. You can only access the island by boat.

Antique Snowmobile Museum (Northern Timber Cruisers)
northerntimbercruisers.com/antique-snowmobile-museum.htm

Millinocket Road, Millinocket. Sledders will appreciate the collection of antique snowmobiles, exhibits, and photos. The museum is next to the Timber Cruisers' clubhouse, off Millinocket Road.

Millinocket Historical Society Museum
millinockethistoricalsociety.org/museum/

Located at 80 Central Street, Millinocket. Check the website for hours.

Millinocket Memorial Library
millinocketmemoriallibrary.org

The library, at 5 Maine Avenue, hosts programs, events, and more. Check the website for hours.

Millinocket Pool and Playground
millinocket.org/community/recreationpool/

At Katahdin Pride Park, 199 State Street, you'll find a playground, tennis courts, and outdoor pool and bathhouse that includes a kiddie pool, intermediate pool, deep pool with diving board, and water slide.

Patten Lumbermen's Museum
lumbermensmuseum.org
6 Shin Pond Road, Patten
(207) 528-2650
Visit this museum for an authentic look into Maine's logging history, complete with stories from river drivers, logging camp artifacts, and much more. The Lumbermen's Museum has seasonal hours; check the website for dates and times.

PLANE TRIPS

Currier's
curriersflyingservice.com/scenic-tours/
Based in Greenville Junction, Currier's offers a Mount Katahdin tour.

Katahdin Air
katahdinair.com
Based on Ambajejus Lake, this air service company specializes in seaplane fly-ins and offers scenic plane trips of varying lengths.

WHITEWATER RAFTING
Several outfitters run trips of all lengths, for all ages and abilities, on the Penobscot River.

New England Outdoor Center (NEOC)
neoc.com

Northern Outdoors
northernoutdoors.com

Penobscot River Rafting and Tubing
penobscotrivertubing.com

Three Rivers Rafting
threeriverswhitewater.com/penobscot-river-rafting

Places To Stay

BAXTER | SOUTHERN SECTION

Big Moose Inn Cabins and Campground
bigmoosecabins.com

Lodge, cabins, and camping, as well as a restaurant and bar, on Millinocket Lake near Baxter State Park's Togue Gatehouse entrance.

New England Outdoor Center
neoc.com

Upscale cabins and lodges, near South Baxter/Togue Gatehouse entrance, on the shores of Millinocket Lake; the River Drivers Restaurant is open to the public for lakeside dining.

New England Outdoor Center's Penobscot Outdoor Center
neoc.com/penobscot-outdoor-center

Camping, cabin tents, and bunkhouse just before the South Baxter/Togue Gatehouse entrance; the Broken Paddle Pub serves food and drinks, picnic table–style.

Katahdin Lake Wilderness Camps
katahdinlakewildernesscamps.com

Adventure lodge with shorefront cabins; lies within Baxter State Park but is managed privately. You can only get there by plane or a 3-plus-mile hike.

Wilderness Edge Campground
wildernessedgecampground.com

Tent and RV camping and cabins near Baxter State Park's Togue Gatehouse entrance.

DEBSCONEAG LAKES WILDERNESS AREA

Abol Campground and Store
abolcampground.com
facebook.com/abolbridge

Camping near the southern part of Baxter State Park and the Debsconeag Lakes Wilderness Area.

Chewonki's Big Eddy Cabins and Campground
bigeddy.chewonki.org

Tent sites, cabin rentals, and RV camping on the western edge of Baxter State Park, at Mile 28.5 on the Golden Road.

Penobscot River Corridor Campsites, Maine Bureau of Parks and Lands
www1.maine.gov/cgi-bin/online/doc/parksearch/details.pl?park_id=84

Horserace Brook, Salmon Falls, Abol Pines, Abol Falls, and a few other backcountry campgrounds are located along the Golden Road, with sites available on a first-come, first-served basis, for a small fee ($6 for Maine residents; $12 for nonresidents; call 207-941-4014 for more information).

BAXTER | NORTHERN SECTION

Mt. Chase Lodge
1517 Shin Pond Road, Mount Chase
mtchaselodge.com

Lodge, private cabins, restaurant, and recreational activities on Upper Shin Pond in Mount Chase.

Shin Pond Village
shinpond.com

Tent sites, cabin rentals, RV camping, with a general store, restaurant, and other amenities, in Mount Chase near Baxter State Park's Matagamon Gate entrance.

KATAHDIN WOODS AND WATERS NATIONAL MONUMENT

Bowlin Camps Lodge
bowlincamps.com

Cabin rentals and a lodge on the East Branch of the Penobscot River, near Katahdin Woods and Waters National Monument.

Food, Supplies, & More

Abol Campground and Store
abolcampground.com/
facebook.com/abolbridge

Closest place for provisions near Debsconeag Lakes Wilderness Area, on the Golden Road.

Ellis Family Market
ellisfamilymarket.com

Last place for provisions before entering Baxter State Park at the Matagamon Gatehouse.

Katahdin Kritters
katahdinkritters.com

Pet care for your four-legged friends who can't come along!

North Woods Trading Post
nwoodstradingpost.com

Last place for provisions before entering Baxter State Park via the Togue Gatehouse.

ACKNOWLEDGMENTS

The Katahdin region is an amazing area filled with wonderful people, and many of these wonderful people were a great help in the creation of this book, providing suggestions for kid-friendly hikes and information about specific hikes or areas, and by generally offering support for the book's creation and dissemination. These wonderful people include Aaron Megquier and Friends of Baxter State Park; Andy Bossie, Darron Collins, Ken Olson, Don Hudson, and Friends of Katahdin Woods and Waters; Wende Sairio and the Katahdin Area Chamber of Commerce; Matt Polstein, the New England Outdoor Center, and Katahdin Area Trails; Jessica Masse; and Tricia Cyr at Moose Drop In.

Thanks must go as well to Melissa Kim and Teresa Lagrange at Islandport Press for their vision, helping to turn Hattie's journal entries and a collection of maps into such a compelling, kid-friendly guide, and just for putting up with me! And thank you, Jada Fitch, for your beautiful sketches. They have turned this guide book into a work of art.